Courageous HOPE

The Call of Leadership

LEONARD DOOHAN

PAULIST PRESS
New York / Mahwah, NJ

Cover and book design by Lynn Else

Library of Congress Cataloging-in-Publication Data

Doohan, Leonard.
    Courageous hope : the call of leadership / Leonard Doohan.
      p. cm.
    Includes bibliographical references.
    ISBN 978-0-8091-4727-4 (alk. paper)
    1. Leadership—Religious aspects—Christianity. 2. Hope—Religious aspects—Christianity. I. Title.
    BV4597.53.L43D65 2011
    253—dc22

                                                              2011009875

Published by Paulist Press
997 Macarthur Boulevard
Mahwah, New Jersey 07430

www.paulistpress.com

Printed and bound in the
United States of America

CONTENTS

Contents

I dedicate this book to our daughter, Eve-Anne, and
her husband, Kevin, with all my love.
With continued gratitude to my wife, Helen, for all her help in
reading, correcting, and editing, as well as for her
many suggestions throughout the writing of this book.

INTRODUCTION
The Need of Hope

RECENT events in the United States and elsewhere indicate the hunger for hope and change felt by so many people from all walks of life. They want different kinds of leaders and a different vision of the future. Ours is a time to refocus the nature of leadership; it is a time for leaders to listen to a different call. People are yearning for leaders who will serve the common good and bring about a future worth living for. Certainly not all leaders will answer this call, but perhaps a few will and thereby bring about the longed-for change. The need is great. The world is desperate for leaders of hope.

We have gone through a trying decade in leadership. So many leaders today work in situations of ambiguity, tension, and often despair ("despair" comes from Latin and means "no hope"). They see failed leadership all around them, incompetent politicians, irresponsible boards, and greedy CEOs. In the eyes of many, today's leaders fail to cope with the big issues, have lost people's confidence, and are disliked by people. Our world of leadership is depressing; it lacks accountability. So-called leaders burden their followers with their incompetence and then leave, and fear is made systemic. We are surrounded with wars, economic failures, organizational disasters, immorality, political processes that do not work, and a loss of meaning in many organizations we had formerly cherished—all the result of failed leadership. Many followers just do not believe it can get any worse; people are losing resilience and vitality. There is a loss of hope and even a renunciation of hope among young people, and some people's unconscious attitudes block hope. "The cynics are winning.

1

People are fed up, angry, disgusted, and pessimistic about their future. Alienation is higher than it has been in a quarter-century. Loyalty to institutions—and institutions' loyalty to people—is sinking like a stone."[1] No one can lead when surrounded with so much negativity toward leadership, but we must find and cultivate leaders of hope who can move us in a new direction, inspire us, and draw us to a worthwhile future, thereby giving meaning to our present and provoking a hope for change.

Many people turn the aggression they feel inward to depression and abuse; in oppression they cry out for liberation that only hope can bring. In the past we considered burnout among leaders; today we have burnout among followers. Many consider their so-called leaders as terminally incompetent and feel stressed by their continued lack of leadership. Others in desperation place unrealistic expectations on shallow leaders, offering them uncritical admiration. This often results in leaders becoming arrogant, controlling, elitist, and manipulative. Many leaders are impoverished, weak, and wounded; some feel guilt and fear for their failures, and others live in an atmosphere of oppression and intimidation. Others remain in a state of denial about the effects of their abysmal decisions. Many work hard and pour out their best efforts for little appreciation, lots of opposition, and few positive results. Many leaders must guard against cynicism, burnout, and depression. Contemporary organizational life is frequently a robber of inner peace for leader and follower alike, for both are starved of hope. These situations destroy inspirational values of leadership, deadening or destroying the enthusiasm that strengthens leadership, and gnawing at any hope of change.

Many so-called leaders bring about death, not life, to individuals and their hopes, to organizations and their common endeavors. Leaders often seem paralyzed by the existing order and do not know how to activate a new one. They talk endlessly about the future and do nothing about it. They have blinders on that let them see just a little, while the vision of hope is outside their focus. What we are left with is "skilled incompetence" where leaders protect themselves from the challenges of the future.[2] Their patient endurance is unlit by hope. Many of the qualities needed in leadership today are not those that are conducive to advancement in one's career. In all this hopelessness, good leaders see something beyond the anguish and tyranny of help-lessness. First they must protect themselves from being changed by the hopelessness around them; in the middle of it all they can still live complex lives with a great deal of integrity and generosity.

The leader of hope who bypasses the outmoded models of aggressive and dominant leadership from the past must still face the oppression that comes with frustrated hopes—his or her own or fol-lowers'. He or she will need to work with people who show indiffer-ence, cold-heartedness, and arid or unproductive ideas of old. He or she must promote alternative leadership structures that reinforce ded-ication to a vision of hope, establish a culture of trust, try and test what is different, and welcome alternative ways of collaborating. We do not need more leadership; we need a different approach to leadership. Our leaders have disheartened us, and it is depressing to look at the future that many of our current leaders are likely to produce. Many books on leadership are written to help students be the best of what leaders have been. We do not need more of what we have had. We no longer need leaders produced by organizations, but leaders with human integrity, spirit, and heart—leaders of hope who bring their hope to the organization and find and fulfill other people's hopes. Many books are filled with practical suggestions; but rather than practical recommendations, leaders need a different vision and under-standing of their role in the world and a different sense of destiny. We need to wake up and realize it is useless to improve the system we have; it does not work.

It is no longer enough to solve problems with yesterday's think-ing; a leader must create something new.[3] It is no longer enough to react to crisis; we need to respond to the future in hope. Leading in the same old way will produce the same old results. We hear so often

3

that we live in times of great change, but it is just moderate change in comparison with the real change that a vision of hope will bring. Many get enthusiastic about sprinkling their mission with assorted values, but hope will bring a totally different value system. Leaders of hope must discard all forms of pressure or manipulation, show benevolence to all, and act with others collaboratively. They seek a better world and a better organization within that world, and rejoice in partial successes on the road. They work for the greater good, trying to satisfy their own and others' yearnings for fulfillment. They feel responsible for others' shared hopes and endeavor to meet them in cooperation with others. They must be enthused by the vision of hope, but work with it in humility. They cannot impose it on others; otherwise they simply substitute their own dictatorship for someone else's. Organizations everywhere are desperate for leaders of hope.

We are immersed in cries of desperation from those who hunger for good, decent, ethical, hopeful leadership instead of the greed, bullying, selfishness, disregard of others' rights, unpunished crimes, and misplaced priorities that we have seen. We cannot go on with the hopeless leadership of the incompetent and neglectful. We must move beyond the anguish and tragic sense of loss and invest in leaders of hope. This book addresses the kind of leaders we need in order to face tomorrow with dignity, integrity, and hope. Leaders who will have prophetical, mystical, charismatic, and healing effects on society will bring a new generation of hopefulness.

CHAPTER ONE

THE NATURE OF HOPE

LEADERS who strive to engage people in the pursuit of excellence must themselves be inspired and highly motivated, as well as inspiring and motivating others. Often it is a particular vision, or simply a set of practical goals, or a unique complex of strategies that somehow enthuses others to pursue the excellence the leader places before them. I propose that more than anything else it is a vision of hope that can excite and empower leaders to inspire others to strive for a common vision. Decisions of great leaders are made in light of this ultimate vision and goal of humanity. These leaders of hope will still need to keep their feet on the ground, be skilled administrators, and be inspired and creative community visionaries. However, their task is to transform society. Inspired managers transform organizations, leaders transform people one at a time, and impact society as a whole, leading it to a vision of promise, and they do this within the context of organizational success and development.

The vision of hope that is the primary motivator of exceptional leadership consists of more than developing futuring skills of leadership. It is a faith-filled vision of our hopes for humanity as a whole and for each individual in particular. This hope reveals who we are called to be, and it opens our hearts to the promises of God. Then, such hope challenges us to live in light of this future in which we believe. This leader of hope matures his or her leadership through the struggles and adversity encountered in striving to implement and anticipate this vision of hope.

1. HOPE REVEALS WHO WE ARE

Hope is a leader's conviction of what the future will be like and should be like. It implies a dynamic commitment, a passionate pursuit of the better future that is foreseen, and so hope is never passive. For a gifted leader, hope is a way of looking at reality, a kind of perception, an insight into possibilities, and an understanding of what will happen. Hope is not a dream, but it is the basic attitude that makes all dreams possible. When we become aware of ourselves as incomplete human beings, open to betterment, and called to fulfillment, then immediately we are filled with hope. Hope is about the meaning of life, about what it means to be human. It is the foundation of a desire for transformation, the awareness that things will be different than they are. For a leader, hope is the conviction that we are being drawn to a new and greater reality.

Leaders know that the past is never decisive for a great present; the future is. The unborn future may lie in the past, and we can anticipate a fulfilled past in the future, but it is always hope that gives a meaningful expression to life in the present. Hope is greater than the accumulation of memories, for no matter how great they are, the reality they represented has disappeared. The past may be prologue, but the leader of hope shuns the past and looks with conviction to the future. It always implies resiliency and openness, for hope-filled visions evolve, and we must struggle to fulfill them. However, the object of hope is not yet present to us and so cannot be the object of confidence. Rather, hope can be transformed into reality, even when hope seems beyond reason, when we are convinced of the future in faith.

I believe that hope is a forgotten virtue, a discarded energy of the human spirit, and a lost dimension of life. However, a great leader perceives that hope is critical to human development, for when a human being has no hope, everything falls apart, every other virtue and quality suffers. Without hope people are paralyzed, and they live in the hell of hopelessness, as Dante suggested when above the gates of hell he placed the sign "Abandon hope, all you who enter here" (*Inferno*, Canto III). The future for which we hope gives meaning to all present reality. Hope is the greatest motivator of human development and of leadership in particular. "Man [or woman] lives in so far as he [or she] has aspirations and plans, that is to say, in so far as he [or she] hopes."[1]

Human beings instinctively hope. It is part of human nature to yearn, to search for fullness of life, to create a future about which people can be enthusiastic. It is part of human existence to hope, and men and women discover and realize their hopes in interaction with the world. "The task of transforming the world is inseparable from [a person's] absolute responsibility for perfecting self; it is a mission entrusted to him [or her]."[2] However, a person's daily efforts never seem to realize all that he or she yearns for. "[A person's] capacity for hope always proves larger than his [or her] hopes in isolation; his [or her] future inevitably transcends all his [or her] concrete realizations of them."[3] Leaders understand that men and women carry within themselves the desire to be who they are capable of being, and leaders must not neglect these yearnings of hope. But the hope we speak about in this book is more than that.

Hope is the most basic attitude of Christian faith. A person has faith in what he or she hopes for. "Now faith is the assurance of things hoped for, the conviction of things not seen" (Heb 11:1). Hope is rooted in faith and is the proof of belief. "It is through faith that a man [or woman] finds the path of true life, but it is only hope that keeps him [or her] on that path."[4] Leaders of hope do not accept other people, organizations, or situations as they are, but see what they can become and courageously and perseveringly make decisions in light of what they hope for. Heraclitus pointed out, "He who does not hope for what is beyond expectation will not find it."

Hope, insofar as it is the concrete expression of faith, cannot be reduced to expectations or to what is merely realizable or possible, or even to an unenlightened utopia. Moreover, the hope of faith is not the accumulation of easily attained individual hopes or what you yearn for when you are at your best. We are not talking about people who hope for this or for that. The hoped-for vision that determines how we live in the present is the vision of life with God. This is the reality behind what we believe that challenges the way we live in the present. "Now hope that is seen is not hope. For who hopes for what is seen? But if we hope for what we do not see, we wait for it with patience" (Rom 8:24–25). So this hope reveals the greater truth of a person and what he or she really believes. It explains the ultimate meaning of life and therefore informs how we deal with the present. Leaders who understand this can motivate others to greatness. For Christians, Jesus' resurrection to new life is an affirmation of the future and a passage to a new hope that changes the way we live in the present.

The object of hope implies knowledge, for it is not guesswork or the arrival of the unexpected. It includes a commitment to community, for it is not solitary or isolationist. It stresses an appreciation of history, especially salvation history, for it is the hope of humanity, not of some individual. It includes awareness of sin and human weakness, for it is not a utopian ideal. It focuses on ultimate hope in union with God in freedom from everlasting death, for it is not the good but minor hopes of each day. It is a gift of God to faith-filled dedication, for it is not something men and women can attain by themselves. Hope does not give us peace and satisfaction, but it causes unrest, impatience, restlessness, and dissatisfaction as one faces self, others, and a world in need of transformation. We cannot reconcile ourselves with what we see, but only with what we hope will be achieved as part of the vision of God.

So while faith gives rise to hope, hope is God's gift to men and women, and the language of religion is generally the language of hope,[5] for it speaks of newness of life for individuals and redemptive liberation for the whole of creation. Hope gives us glimpses beyond the normal horizons of life into an afterlife that conditions how we live in this one. As a result of this insight into the horizons of hope, our transcendental hope challenges us to make ourselves into who we are capable of being through daily decisions and choices. We realize our hope for the vision of God in daily activity, and the daily future we create makes the ultimate future a reality as we live it and grow into it through patience and fortitude.

Leadership begins with a spiritual journey into the depths of one's heart and inner convictions, where alone one hears a call that no one else hears. This call is first of all to transform oneself and one's role in the world and then to reach out to contribute to the transformation of others, individually and in society. It is common to speak about a leader's inner spirit and motivation, but the primary motivating attitude of a leader is hope. There is no great leadership without self-transformation. Each leader develops his or her life based on core values, but these values are part of the vision of hope. Hope is not a skill set, although it will require new skills. It is not a leadership style, but it can be effective with several and not effective with others. It is not a theory of leadership. Hope is the inner motivation of a leader, the fundamental modifier of leadership style. Everything else can be a technique, including faith (when it is generally interpreted as a belief system) and even love. Hope cannot be a technique, although talking about hope can be, as we have seen in several political processes.

Hope reflects the true inner convictions of a person. It results from conversion and is proof of faith. Individuals and organizations that look to the past or extrapolate from the present are destined to fail in leadership, whereas the great leader looks to the future in hope, dedicates self to moral renewal, focuses on the essential human values contained in the orientation of hope, and motivates and mobilizes others to attain the new vision of hope. For such a person hope is the source of life, as it is the source of leadership.

2. HOPE OPENS OUR HEARTS TO A GOD OF PROMISE

What people believe in, they hope for. If they did not hope for the object of their faith, then the latter would be empty words. We believe that at the end of this age we will participate in the age to come. So it is that Christianity for sure, and other religions too, speak of the promised land, the kingdom that will come, the future reign of God, a new creation, the universal resurrection, forgiveness, and redemption. "By awesome deeds you answer us with deliverance, O God of our salvation; you are the hope of all the ends of the earth and of the farthest seas" (Ps 65:5). These are the components of hope, and we cling to this hope because God is a God of promise, not an empty promise but one we are convinced will be real. "Through hope, faith avoids the mistake of taking the hiddenness of God for absence."[6] The daily work of leaders evolves within this context, and they make their decisions in light of this vision. This hope makes faith real. "May the God of hope fill you with all joy and peace in believing, so that you may abound in hope by the power of the Holy Spirit" (Rom 15:13).

Of course, God brings about this new creation in which we place our hope (see Ps 33:22). We cannot produce it ourselves, but we can live guided by that end-time vision and thus participate in it and anticipate it in our present lives. In this way, what we claim to believe in, and thus hope for, becomes real. "See, I am making all things new" (Rev 21:5). Thus, God's future, which is our hope, overwhelms and overcomes the depressing misery of our world. God's future trans-forms our present. "Our hope for solving problems in our personal lives and in the world is not based on confidence in our own ability or on a dangerous mixture of technological knowledge and political domination. Our hope is in God's concern for the mending of society and all creation."[7]

However, the way leaders conceive of God's future affects the way they live now. Some believers consider that God's promise of a

new heaven and a new earth is absolutely future and totally unconnected with the present. They are convinced that no matter what we
do in the present, it has no effect on the future for which we hope.
Others focus so much on the saving in-breaking of God in human life
that no importance can be given to what happens before or after.
Hope is realized in the existential moment of grace. Still others see
hope achieved exclusively by the Savior whose personal intervention
realizes the end-promise for each individual. In such a view, our contributions amount to nothing. In the last half century, it has been common to view the realization of hope as a combination of awe-inspired
appreciation of God's final gift in the reign of hope with the reality of
human belief shown in the dedication to make that reign real and
anticipate it in the present.[8] We can say that "God is already present
in the way in which [the] future masters the present because [the]
future decides what becomes of the present."[9] In this view we live out
our beliefs because God is our hope, and we live out the beginnings
of each day in light of the promise of the end. "Christians must be
driven by transformative action....Christians expect more of
humankind because God expects more."[10] Hope is essentially based
on Jesus' life and teachings (see Eph 1:9–10). Jesus reveals who we are
and who we are called to be. So the values to which Jesus calls us must
permeate our own lives and communities.

God's hoped-for gift of redemption, "the introduction of a better
hope, through which we approach God" (Heb 7:19), is not something
just left to the end of time. Our hope urges us to action in the present.
So we speak about human involvement in liberation as a form of solidarity and an aspect of dedicated hope. "The expression of this basic
primordial hope is to be found in the human, historical hopes of the
world such as the promotion of justice, the establishment of human
rights, the pursuit of happiness, the care of the earth, and a commitment to social and political reform—without, however, being reduced
to any one of these particular expressions."[11] As these human efforts
become inadequate or stunted by sin, we again open ourselves to

God's grace, and so we see that all human efforts are necessary, but only anticipate God's own vision of hope for us all.

The gift of hope as a theological virtue means we hope in God or for God. This is part of the dynamism of a Christian personality; because of grace we live in hope. "The LORD is my portion, says my soul, therefore I will hope in him" (Lam 3:24). Hope is a moral virtue that implies obligations on the believer who must live in light of the hope in which he or she claims to believe. Hope is a charism in some individuals, enabling them to motivate others with their enthusiasm for what can lie ahead. Hope is also a spiritual energy that moves individuals to involve the whole self in attaining the goals of hope. When these various aspects of hope come together, the end transforms every day. "Human beings are God's great love. Human beings are [God's] dream for [the] earthly world. Human beings are [God's] image for the earth [God] loves. God created everything in finished form, but...created human beings in hope."[12]

The problem of a leader's spirituality and human activity in the present world depends on how he or she sees the relationship between the human spirit and the absolute end in God. The fact that God is a God of promise means the faithful lovingly commit themselves to live in "the hope of righteousness" (Gal 5:5). "In its hope, love surveys the open possibilities of history. In love, hope brings all things into the light of the promises of God."[13] Moreover, the end we see in hope is not just the transformation of humanity but also the reconciliation of societies, and the liberation and harmony of all creation. In other words, our hope is that the whole of reality will be healed and brought into union.[14] This vision is the promise of God, the object of our hope, and the sphere of our spiritual commitment. "Hope does not disappoint us, because God's love has been poured into our hearts through the Holy Spirit that has been given to us" (Rom 5:5). The awesome and overwhelming love of God calls us to live out our lives in the presence of people, institutions, events, and creation, all longing for transformation, all already transformed in our hope. "The notion which, already in the Bible, sums up the authentic way in which the believer behaves in history has only one name, hope, because hoping is the act which links the present both to the fixed point of the historical Jesus and to the eschatological (end of time) vanishing point."[15]

When we think about what we believe and the hope that lies ahead in the promise of God, in other words, that our "faith and hope are set on God" (1 Pet 1:21), we discover two aspects of this vision. First, it includes the fulfillment of all that we yearn for as human beings: to live without threats to peace, free from our own inadequacies, saved from weaknesses and sin that make us less than we want to be. It finds satisfaction, pleasure, and joy in life, and respect and fulfillment in a meaningful life. It welcomes us as an integral part of community, sharing mutual love, and discovering the enrichment of life together. So we want to discover that we can be the best we are capable of being. Second, we hope to benefit from experiences beyond our expectations, we presume we will be surprised, we feel life will be more than we ever thought, and we hope to be transformed in union with God. Humanity is divided into two groups: those whose hopes are limited and end with the end of this world and those whose hopes are intimately linked to the vision of a world to come. Leaders of hope open their hearts to a God of promise. They can never be satisfied with mediocrity, but must always pursue the excellence of hope, struggling each day to anticipate tomorrow's hopes. When we say that all authority is from God, which is a statement of hope, it changes the way in which men and women lead others.

3. HOPE CHALLENGES US TO LIVE IN LIGHT OF THE FUTURE

The only real question for human beings is what will happen at the end of life. The way we view the end in hope can revolutionize how we deal with the present. If we make the end-time irrelevant, we make our lives meaningless and irrelevant too. Hoping in God's promise is a belief in God's involvement in development and history. "For surely I know the plans I have for you, says the LORD, plans for your welfare and not for harm, to give you a future with hope" (Jer 29:11). Hope has become this-worldly. Nowadays, writers emphasize "the revolutionary potential of hope," and that "Christian hope is directive, uplifting, and critical. It revolutionizes and transforms the present."[16] If leaders know what they hope for, they will be dissatisfied with society, its structures, and its relationships. Our hope is a judgment on the failure and inadequacies of the past, the present, and the future without God (see Isa 43:18–19). We look to the future with conviction, and in the promise of God we see a vision of justice, community, and mutuality in relationships.

Faith means being committed to hope. Hope becomes a way of approaching the present because of what we believe in the future. We live in spiritual tension between "the already" and "the not yet." "So, if any one is in Christ, there is a new creation; everything old has passed away; see, everything has become new!" (2 Cor 5:17). So our hope demands that we live responsibly in the modern world. "At every level the New Testament espouses a 'there and then' perspective in order to say something about the 'here and now.'"[17] Nowadays, hope for the promises of God in the afterlife has become hope for the world as an anticipation of the afterlife. "Human history must become the locus for the provisional realization of Christian hope for salvation."[18] Put another way, hope should make us creative in dealing with the present and challenge us to create a desirable future in the present, not just for ourselves but for others too, for hope is always a shared hope. Hope is a way of living one's faith and love. "As long as hope does not embrace and transform the thought and action of men [and women], it remains topsy-turvy and ineffective. Hence Christian eschatology [discourse about the end of time] must make the attempt to introduce hope into worldly thinking, and thought into the believing hope."[19] What is "there and then" inspires us to develop a "here and now."

Frequently we see thought of the afterlife as a distraction from involvement in the present. However, the way we dedicate ourselves to the transformation of the present is more determined by how we view the afterlife than by anything else. Hope for the future does not despise the "now" of the present. Rather, it sees now as part of the hoped-for future, a step on the way. Living in hope is the best way to give fullness to the present moment, for genuine hope is optimism filled with realism (see John 16:33).

So the future becomes real in the life of a hope-filled leader who sees present dedication as a participation in the truth of the future. However, this hope is never merely individual, for the object of hope is communal; God's promise is for the whole human community (see Eph 4:4). Men and women work together to attain their hope, each person looking to others as integral to his or her own development. "For this reason, as I must hope for myself, so must I for him [or her] and he [and she] for me: we must hope for all of us. This call to hope, which is both common to and yet higher than all of us because it transcends each and every one of us, reveals the basis which is common to and yet higher than all: the call of a transcendent future."[20] Hope gives rise to the duty to peace, justice, and human development. Individuals may have competing small hopes. But the hoped-for future is a shared, common hope for which we work together in love. "It is that virtue by which we take responsibility for the future, not simply our individual future but the future of the world."[21] We work together to implement hope. We may well start with all the small hopes of each day, but the true believer's hope is a part of a vision of life, a philosophy of life, a way of approaching life. "Christian hope is not opposed to the hopes of this world. All these hopes are rather the means through which the one hope is mediated. Man [or woman] meets God's future by facing his [or her] worldly future. Here Christian hope co-ordinates, criticizes and gathers together the hopes of this world, rises above them, and fulfills them when they reach their limit."[22]

Courageous Hope

Hope gives meaning to the present and challenges us to live in light of the future. In fact, hope is intimately connected with death and calls leaders to make decisions in the context of their own deaths. In such a vision, hope means bringing out the best in yourself and in every person with whom you work and in every part of your organization. Changing the present to reflect the future is the task of a great leader who understands his or her interconnectedness with everyone else. When leaders without hope look to the past and the present to find meaning and direction amid the incomprehensibility, they are thwarted. Leaders with hope, grounded in a vision of the future, find challenge, direction, common identity, and connections that lead to common hope, spiritual renewal, and unending challenge. Nothing brings greater clarity to life than death. "That is why faith, wherever it develops into hope, causes not rest but unrest, not patience but impatience."[23] One author, commenting on the quote from the first letter of Peter that we must always be ready to give an account of the hope that lies within us, points out that there is a difference between the hope and the account. The latter is not the hope itself. We must defend our hope, and we do that by the life that we live individually and in organizations. The same author calls for "a hope with its feet on the ground, a worldly hope, it must be a social critique of the world."[24] He later draws a powerful conclusion applicable to those Christians who wish to be leaders: "Without a concrete strategy, however, love and hope are shapeless. They become merely-believed-in discipleship, merely-believed-in love, and merely-believed-in hope."[25]

The leader of confident hope can respond with humility and become a servant leader of a shared hope, giving to others reasons for living and reasons for hoping amid the pressures of modern life. "Always be ready to make your defense to anyone who demands from you an accounting for the hope that is in you" (1 Pet 3:15). The vision of hope reflects the basic elements for a leader's program of action. "Let us hold fast to the confession of our hope without wavering, for [God] who has promised is faithful" (Heb 10:23). This is God's vision for the welfare of humanity, a program of action for human beings in their personal and institutional renewal.

4. HOPE MATURES THROUGH ADVERSITY

Hope is based on the convictions of faith. It is not empirically verifiable, but we must "seize the hope set before us" (Heb 6:18). Hope is a risk. It requires trust. Since a common hope is also a common risk, it needs patience to keep the hope alive, and it insists on humility to let go of failed hopes and move on.

Among the many false or inadequate forms of hope are self-righteous confidence on the one hand and a superficial belief in progress on the other. Some hopes are empty and actually represent a form of depression concerning the future. Thus we use the vocabulary of hope to cover our hopelessness. "Let's hope that this or that will happen" frequently expresses anxiety, and hope cannot coexist with doubt. When people tell us, "Oh, be realistic!" they tend and intend to put a damper on our hope. Others' insistence that "it doesn't work; we've tried it!" likewise hampers our move forward. Unquestionably, hope is a risk, for we can set ourselves up for short-term failure of the small hopes that form part of the larger vision of hope. But hope must remain when hopes fail.

Fearful leaders and their organizations threaten hope when they betray us by their absorption in depressing outlooks, focused on the greed of immediate gain or the criminality of abusive power. Hope is also threatened by *despair*—when people claim there is no future, no meaning, it is too late to do anything, or we cannot change; by *apathy*—when people have no desires, no care, loss of enthusiasm, or accept the status quo; by *shame*—when others are inflicted by humiliation from unfulfilled hopes; by *presumption*—by those who insist they know everything already, they have done it before, they know best; or by boring *surrender* to what we already have—claiming it is fine, we can survive, we have our niche, we should not rock the boat. People with these defensive and frustrating positions are without hope and have no future and no faith. Their future is a prolongation of the present, and their faith is the re-articulation of the past.

All the above are the trials of hope. The theology of hope cannot be separated from the cross or from suffering. We live in a world that found the cross to be an appropriate response to the hope of Christ. There can be no hope without adversity, but filled with faith, we must walk through "the door of hope" (Hos 2:15), for we are "prisoners of hope" (Zech 9:12). Gregory of Nyssa, an early Christian writer, assured us: "The power of God is capable of finding hope where hope no longer exists and a way where the way is impossible." So in a world of fear we must maintain an ardent hope, help other people find the path of hope, and overcome difficulties in the hope of better days. "Hope and the kind of thinking that goes with it consequently cannot submit to the reproach of being utopian, for they do not strive after things that have 'no place,' but after things that have 'no place as yet,' but can acquire one."[26]

Hope always implies facing up to suffering, our own and other people's. As we strive to implement a vision of hope, we must confront the common human experience of suffering. We must interrupt "any ignoring of human suffering, all suppression of human value. Without the edges of grief and hope," our efforts become empty and destroy authentic hope.[27] Hope is always communal, and hoping for others means drawing them out of suffering, whatever form it takes. "Christian discipleship offers as its hope human solidarity rather than domination. It is founded on a hope that the human heart will turn outward."[28] So hope includes compassion and solidarity. In fact, hope is not only an expression of faith but also of Christian love.

"Most of us forget—or perhaps never knew—that hope lay at the bottom of Pandora's box. Usually we just remember that all the troubles flew out. The story is important because it reminds us that even in the midst of these troubles, hope remains."[29] So, for a believer the object of hope is not only the resurrection after death, but the experience of hope is also made up of the mini-resurrections of every day after the mini-deaths of each day. For a leader, living in hope is stressful, for he or she is never satisfied and is always in tension to something more and better. Saying "no" to a tested present and "yes" to the future is risky. Such a leader maintains hope when the hopes of each day fail, and maintains optimism since pessimism is an expression of despair and nonhope.

Grounded in experience, hope emerges from the deprivation, loss, and emptiness of life. This is the task that lies before a great leader: to abandon the past and to move forward to a vision of hope. Thus for each leader, hope matures through the spiritual journey from self-absorption in the false securities of the past to self-transcendence in the faith-filled vision of promise. This is a journey that cannot be made in isolation, for hope is communal and includes community relationships. Building this communal vision of hope has its own trials, for you cannot argue or persuade people into hope. It requires the support of others: friends and companions in a common vision, and then it attracts us and compels us to action. By excluding extremes and by sustaining hope in others, a leader can begin to create a community of hope.

CHAPTER TWO

LEADERS GUIDED BY HOPE

HOPE is the key motivating factor of a leader's life. For some people, their leadership role is a job or a career, but for a small number it is a way of being in the world. Hope will never substitute for the skills of management, or for one's chosen style of leadership, with all the knowledge, skills, behaviors, and vision each requires. For a great leader, his or her vision of hope is an overlay on all else, a modifier of all one does, and the motivation for one's way of being and living in this world. For a great leader, everything in life is colored by hope—call, purpose, destiny, and vision of leadership.

1. A DIFFERENT UNDERSTANDING OF CALL

A leader of hope feels *called to make decisions in light of the vision of hope*. The leader of hope sees his or her leadership as being guided by the future rather than the present. To lead has always meant being the chief figure in a group, having the needed knowledge, going first, guiding, showing the way, and influencing the actions of others. Leaders could do all this because of their power, coercion, pay-offs, influence, inspiration, confidence, and charisma. Since leadership has always been so important to humanity, many people have studied it for centuries, giving us a variety of images, symbols, models, and theories of leadership. These generally depend on interactions between the person of the leader, the goals to be achieved, the interactions of followers, and the various situations encountered. While these four elements are always important, for the leader of hope the point of departure for an understanding of leadership is outside these four. It is the ideal of hope or the vision of promise for humanity that determines the call of the leader, the goals he or she should set, and how he or she ought to interact with followers and deal with changing situations. The leader of hope values the invisible and intangible more than the empirically verifiable, even though always taking the latter into consideration. A leader of hope is a transformational leader who has a transforming influence on self, others, environments, and social life. The leader's vision, mission, high expectations, intellectual stimulation, personal attention, and consideration all focus on hope.

The leader of hope sees clearly that transformation as a goal of leadership, an inherent element of call, focuses first of all on changing oneself. *The leader perceives his or her call and role within the organization in a new way.* The call includes personal conversion, a radical intention to serve the promised vision, a need to be constantly grounded in the Spirit, a sense of self-motivation, and inspiration. Leading from the future means changing a lot of basic assumptions. The refocusing of one's mind and heart, this redirection of one's actions and priorities, is the inner side of leadership greatness. "It is taking the oath of excellence,"[1] a fundamental option, a passion for what is possible, an existential choice to give oneself to hope. An organization can easily survive without a leader's management skills, for others will have them, but no longer without the leader reinventing self through conversion and mature discipleship, through the discovery of a new sense of identity built on the inner self. For the leader of hope, integrity means matching leadership with the vision of hope and promise that the leader accepts in faith.

A leader of hope understands that *the call to leadership now requires new emphases*—vocation, vision, integrity, community building, contemplation, and spirituality. Its foundation is faith, hope, and

21

love as the basis of the personality of a leader of hope, and it manifests its key values in a lived reinterpretation of the eight beatitudes, those eight inward attitudes that highlight the way of life of a leader of hope. In other words, the beatitudes call the leader to be spiritually poor, to undergo life's hardships, to struggle for the world's improvement without complaint, to strive for fulfillment according to the values of God, to be compassionate and merciful, to be single-minded and single-hearted in the way we treat others, to become peacemakers, and to accept the painful consequences of a chosen life (see Matt 5:1–12). As leaders filled with a vision of hope, we need to let our practice of leadership catch up with where our hearts and commitment in faith claim to be. Each one must make hope for the vision of promise real; if one does not have the skills, one is obliged to learn them.

The leader of hope feels called to lead others to share in the hope-filled vision of humanity within the context of their work. The leader of hope sees the service of others as integral to the call and mission, thereby helping each one find a role in the common future vision. The attaining of this vision of hope is now the goal of leadership, and previous goals of leadership are now by-products. Thus excellence of customer service and product quality no longer need the same emphasis as formerly, because they are consequences of facilitating a hope-filled vision of what human interactions ought to be like. A leader of hope has learned how to learn. He or she engages in receptive learning, always open to ideas of anyone who is an integral part of the vision of hope. This person can courageously say, "I have a dream," but immediately asks, "and what are your dreams?" and "what dreams can we build together?"[2]

The leader of hope enables people to live out their own individual calling within the context of their professional lives. Individuals enjoy satisfaction, fulfillment, improved self-concept, and meaningful lives; and issues of productivity, collaboration, and team building become by-products of this vision. The leader of hope knows that for oneself or others, the question of the ultimate meaning of life is part of the struggle-filled purpose of every day. Such a leader feels called to create a working environment where each one can find and develop one's own calling. One's calling is always greater than one's professional life, but the latter can be a significant part of it and a learning situation in which one's calling comes into clearer focus.

The leader of hope's call includes fostering a sense of community within the organization that the leader manages, and does so as a reflection of the vision of promise. There is the hope that love will never be lost. Because of a vision of hope, the leader has faith in others and engages them honestly, welcomes their ideas, and appreciates their integral role within the community. Emphasis on trust, appreciation of each one's role, complementarity, mutuality, and shared responsibility makes it unnecessary to legislate for issues of racism, sexism, harassment, and so on. Once commitment to the vision of hope is made, consequences follow that change the way people relate and make former legislation unnecessary. The leader of hope lives a quality presence to self, others, the world, the job, and God.

The leader of hope always stresses that work is important because of the gifts of the person who does it, not because of what is done. In this understanding there is no such thing as significant work and menial work. *The leader appreciates that every worker is part of the whole vision of humanity*, every one brings dignity to work, and differentiation is not based on type of work but on quality of dedication and responsibility that each one brings to whatever task. In this subjective approach to work, the leader treats every individual within an organization with dignity; no one is merely a means of production. The leader of hope appreciates that this call includes guaranteeing that people come before all else.

The leader of hope acknowledges the need for healing and liberation from whatever forms of suffering or oppression each one faces, so that each one can become who he or she is called to be in hope. In fact, the leader exemplifies a passion for other people's development, a genuine empathy, and an authentic love for each one's healing and

23

growth. The working environment becomes a place of compassion and of concern for each person and his or her needs. The leader will also try to liberate followers from their inability to hope; for many people, hope always looks like too much of a risk. It is also critical that a leader liberates the latent leader that exists within every follower.[3] Furthermore, the leader dedicates self to facing current crises, whether local, regional, or worldwide, striving to liberate the world from visions of the past and the present. All this implies that a leader becomes a model of hope.

The leader of hope knows the importance of bringing out the very best in coworkers. The vision of hope of necessity includes the best of which each one is capable. This will include structuring work time so that it is conducive to reflection, creativity, integration, and fulfillment. It will include delegating and empowering others, collaborating, sharing responsibility, collegiality, and working toward a shared vision. The leader of hope capitalizes on the gifts of each one—from the least qualified to the most creative.

A leader of hope is unable to do anything else except move forward to new realities in spite of constant negativity, professional gripers, and those within the organization who have never seen an issue that they could not grumble about. *A leader faced with problems offers hope as a solution.* A leader of hope feels immersed in a sense of awe and mystery in what the future can become. He or she is dedicated to move away from all forms of self-centeredness and self-embeddedness and move to self-transcendence. The leader wants this for self, for others, and for the organization.

The splendid task of leadership is a vocation to hope. A person without hope is no longer a leader. A great leader is an agent of hope who inspires and energizes others by the vision of hope he or she accepts in faith and works to make real. Becoming a leader of hope is not achieved overnight. It requires faith, positive thinking, sharing with good people, reflection, and contemplation.

2. A CHANGED VIEW
OF LIFE'S PURPOSE

This vocation to be a leader of hope inevitably *means seeing one's own purpose in life in a new way*. The leader of hope sees this call as one of personal transformation to become who he or she is capable of becoming in hope. This call leads to new emphases in leadership and challenges the leader to draw others to share the hope-filled vision. It means enabling people to live out their own calling, fostering a sense of community, and valuing the work of every person. It implies healing and liberation, bringing out the best in everyone, and moving forward in spite of setbacks.

Such a leader sees one's purpose in life as being essentially *a model of hope*.[4] This is more than being an agent of hope, which could be transitory. Being a model is part of one's purpose in life. Hope is the goal of leadership, not a by-product, and this kind of leader acts on hope, encouraging other people's hope, individually in their discretionary commitment and communally in networks of hope. Living out this hope is a form of integrity. These leaders see their unique purpose as managing personal and community hope by being a single-minded and single-hearted presence of hope and wisdom. Their purity of motive is the foundation of their credibility; it is their vision of hope that persuades followers. They know leadership is not based on the exercise of power, nor does it consist in "attitudes of self-importance and narcissism," nor limiting others' spirit of commitment, disengaging others' energy, and emphasizing self-protection and entrenched resistance.[5]

Leaders of hope base their leadership on *appreciating everyone's role in the vision* of hope and on their own personal stature, anchored in hope and lived in principle-centered leadership. One writer suggests three roles of a leader: path finding—discovering the vision, mission, and future; aligning the organization with the vision and future mission; and empowering others to strive for that vision. He

25

further points out that "the person becomes the leader of the future by an inside-out transformation."[6]

This kind of leader sees that part of the purpose in life is to be a leader who *can look at things differently*, looking at everything as if for the first time, and seeing what others do not see. This implies a sense of awe and a spirit of discovery; it means developing imaginative skills of reflection, meditation, and contemplation, so that one can appreciate what others do not, and even foresee the unforeseeable. Part of this ability to see with the eyes of hope is to see the goodness discoverable in everyone and the contribution to a common vision, for "a leader must be able to see people in all of their relationships, in the wholeness of their lives."[7] It also means seeing the whole story in issues under discussion.

A leader of hope appreciates that part of his or her purpose is to *always seek the truth* that emerges from the vision of promise. This truth is outside oneself, it is communal, and it is God's gift. There is no mediocrity in truth, for mediocrity leads to compromises that eat away at the vision of promise. Part of this constant seeking of the truth is to accept the truth about oneself, including one's gifts and weaknesses and even the authority and stature that one has in leadership— accept it and appreciate it, while taking it with a pinch of salt. However, what binds a leader to a group in its search for truth is not authority and stature but a loving bond with others. The truth of the vision of hope must be implemented with patience, honesty, clarity of each one's contribution, experience, and competence. Seeking the truth is complemented by speaking the truth, welcome or unwelcome. Consistency in speaking the truth is part of integrity; it is a way a leader embodies core values for which the leader would die, values that form part of the vision of promise. A leader who seeks the truth and lives with integrity comes across as authentic.

One of the unusual but valuable dimensions of a leader's purpose in life is to *train people to appreciate the importance of emptying themselves of false values*. No one can fill his or her life with a vision of hope when life is already cluttered with false truths, false visions, false missions, and false self. We must break away from the clutter that fills our hearts, our minds, and our souls. We must die to certain forms of superficial life if we are to rise to the fullness of hope. A great leader of hope can raise people above these distractions that block their ability to receive the vision of promise.[8] So a great leader frees others from the domination of causes, social and cultural sin, and the pseudoconvictions of so much of contemporary organizational life. Leaders can help people to empty themselves of false values and free themselves to receive values and vision that really matter.

A leader knows that among his or her primary purposes in life is to *create love, friendship, and community*; love of others is central to leadership today. Love includes service, mentoring, appreciating others' points of view, compassion, and leading others to growth and fulfillment.[9] In practice it includes creating a climate of trust, communication, and caring; thinking with your heart; and loving with your mind. Genuine friendship and love for those who open themselves to a vision of hope mean rooting out of the organization all forms of manipulation, abuse, suppression, and structures of domination. "For most people this experience of friendship and love is the experience that awakens hope in the lives of people; it is especially the experience of love that is unselfish love that empowers and enables people to hope."[10] Such friendship and love lead to a community of hope.

One aspect of a loving community is to encourage the participation of everyone. Part of a leader's purpose is to *interpret the vision of hope in light of other people's intelligent and caring solutions*. This includes solidarity, a willingness to listen to other people's stories, to share their frustrations and pain, and to view things from their perspective. The more followers are informed about the nature of hope, the more critical they can become and less accepting of a single authority figure, since they realize that they too have a role in the vision. The leader can still maintain a role when he or she "is seen as serving the dream and searching for a better one."[11] The leader can encourage others to test and challenge new ideas, foster a sense of belonging, and present them with intermediate visions of hope. "Breakthrough leadership involves developing a shared and compelling vision for what can be, what should be, and what must be. The ability to develop such a vision is contingent on having the ability to embrace what the future may hold."[12] Through all this the leader must live with the tension and anxiety that accompany risk and change. Likewise the leader must show resilience and rededication in the struggle to overcome disappointment and adversity, which are always part of implementing a vision of hope.

3. A NEW SENSE OF DESTINY

Along with a sense of call there need to be several key qualities that make the call realizable, otherwise one's call would always be frustrated. These basic values lead to an enduring purpose. *Such a leader knows that he or she is in this world for a reason.* That purpose in life includes being a model of hope, looking at life differently, seeking the truth, training people to empty themselves of false values, spreading love, creating community, and interpreting the vision of hope for others. Out of this conviction regarding one's purpose in life there emerges a sense of destiny. Such a leader knows that these are responsibilities in this world; this destiny is what makes a leader a model for others.

Every leader of hope feels this sense of destiny. *It is a spiritual awakening* based on core values, ethical commitment, and visioning; a destiny that emerges from call and enduring purpose. Each one has a new sense of identity and self-concept, an awareness of personal accountability for the vision of promise, and a new realization of the importance of humility amid the frailty of life. Leaders know that part of this destiny is to persuade others to live in hope, to constantly strive for what is noble in the vision, and to be worthy of other people's personal hopes. Destiny "means not only effectively leading others through the heroic journey, but also basing their personal lives on the

28

heroic pattern."[13] These leaders have spiritual energy, are enthused by the beauty of ideas, are thrilled at their responsibility to serve others, and are excited at the opportunities of hope. Such leaders of destiny have an unrelenting desire to serve others, an unyielding dedication to high standards, and a yearning to facilitate change that leads to the new vision.

They are spiritual leaders of soul and spirit, whose sense of awe and mystery brings depth to their understanding and love and enables them to live from the inside out. These spiritual leaders of destiny have had *an experience of the mystery of life and of hope*. They struggle to understand it, explain it, proclaim it, share it, and embody it in their lives. Viewing things with the eyes of hope, they discern the power of God in the present for the future. They stand up for the vision they hold, they internalize their values, and without imitating anyone else, they become the leaders they are capable of being—they each become their own person. These individuals who become leaders for humanity have also grasped values beyond the normal horizons of life. They have glimpsed the mystery of God's hope for humanity and feel they have a role of bringing it to fruition.

There is no distinction between leadership and life for great leaders. They are always who they are. The transformation of inner self, the ardent dedication to serve others, and the enthusiastic commitment to build love and community are three facets of the same unique leader and constitute personal spirituality. It goes without saying that a leader must get the job done, whatever the job is. Competence is a prerequisite. No one who is incompetent in the focal issues of work can ever be a great leader. But leadership is more than inspired management, and it starts not with the bottom line or short-term organizational goals but with the vision of hope for humanity. *One's personal destiny implies being faithful to humanity's destiny*. This is a journey for a chosen few, and it is a journey with many dark nights. Integral to this journey is both personal conversion and organizational conversion—facilitating the latter being part of a leader's destiny. The asceticism of living in hope is an ongoing inward journey of purification and self-transcendence. "The longest journey is the journey inward of him [or her] who has chosen his [or her] destiny."[14] This is the journey to inner healing, wisdom, goodness, courage, and confidence. It is above all a journey of self-knowledge, of discovery of one's role in the plan of God. It is a life-changing journey.

The dedication to serve can be described with one word, *magis*. This Latin word means "more," and it catches the depth and quality of the leader's service and sense of destiny. *He or she is always giving "the more."* There is professional commitment; that gift of self that professionals make in the pursuit of professional success. Then there is discretionary commitment; that generous service that goes beyond what is needed to be a good professional and includes the generosity that one is free to give or to withhold. The dedicated service of a leader of hope goes beyond even this in search of more than one would ever expect. Jesus is an example of this kind of service. Paul tells us that Jesus emptied himself to take on the condition of one who serves (Phil 2:17). Several times Jesus claimed he had come among us to serve and not to be served (Matt 20:28; Mark 10:45). During the Last Supper he acted out a prophecy of the purpose of his life when he washed his disciples' feet, as a symbol of his spirit of service (John 13:1–15). His dedication to always give more led him to describe the final stage of self-gift for the healing, growth, and fullness of life for others, when he declared that he would lay down his life for his followers (John 10:15–18).

The leader of hope's enthusiastic commitment to build up love and community can be captured with the idea of *proclaiming a "covenant."* This leader appreciates his or her unifying function. With less concern for personal maintenance, this leader is concerned always with building up the sense of loving community among all followers. "Words such as love, warmth, personal chemistry are certainly pertinent. Covenantal relationships are open to influence. They fill deep needs and they enable work to have meaning and to be fulfilling. Covenantal relationships reflect unity and grace and poise. They are an expression of the sacred nature of relationships."[15] None of these things just happens; the building up of a covenantal relationship needs strategic planning, a readiness to accept criticism from others with acknowledgment of their gifts to community, and humility to recognize one's mistakes and the pain one causes others. Building a covenant needs knowledge, skills, and intense longing for the good of others. More than anything else, covenant refers to God's relationship with people, and a leader of hope sees self as instrumental in this endeavor.

The leader of hope also appreciates that suffering is an integral part of the life of a leader. Generally a person with a sense of destiny has gone through personal suffering and crisis. It is often a source of strength and gives him or her the courage to be a leader of hope. "Tragedy is the author of hope. Crisis brings us face to face with our soul."[16] Now such a leader can be ready for constant change, take success or failure in stride, and face the future with passion, boldness, and courage. The leader can also bear the further pain that comes with hoping when surrounded by people who cannot hope or dream. The leader must accept frustration and defer satisfaction. The leader will need to manage discouragement, depression, and rejection. "Given the pervasiveness of resistance in transformative times, the management of resistance is a required skill for any successful leader today."[17] The leader of hope joyfully accepts the sacrifices of living for hope. This is part of the asceticism of living in hope and is integral to destiny.

Hope calls the leader to enthuse, inspire, unify, and build up others. The destiny of a great leader is to be a spiritual leader, a servant leader, a charismatic leader, a prophet, and a mystic—themes we will see in later chapters.

4. A BREAKTHROUGH INSIGHT INTO LEADERSHIP

We have seen that to be a leader of hope means that one's preparation for leadership is different, one's priorities are different, one's habits, qualities, and virtues are different, one's self-concept is different, and one's attitudes and assumptions are different. One has a different way of looking at life, chooses different alternatives, and makes decisions based on hope. *A leader of hope thinks about leadership in a totally different way.* Hope is not usable as a theory of leadership, but it is a leadership style and a basic set of attitudes with which one approaches leadership. The leader of hope functions in a situation of tension between the already and the not yet. What we see in hope is never the ultimate reality, but it moves us in that direction.

Several authors refer to a new kind of leadership, a "leadership turn," a paradigm shift, a conversion. They suggest that "huge changes are zooming at us," new realities of leadership are emerging, "a new leadership awakening [is] expanding our possibilities," and we have "fundamentally new recipes for comprehending the world of management and leadership." Thus, we can say that "New realities require new approaches to leadership. *Breakthrough leadership is about creating new realities.* New realities call for a whole new way to view the role leaders play in the change process."[18] This new way of viewing the leader's role includes "an ongoing dissatisfaction for what is and an insatiable appetite for realizing potential," and "some rather mysterious aromas that arise from stirrings in things like spirit, heart, and energy." This requires "new health and fresh determination," "the joy of a leadership mind," a spiritual journey of discovery, "an expression of the soul's striving for perfection and transcendence," and a dedication to "pull our future toward us and move into its current."[19] Never have people spoken and written about leadership with the thrill and excitement as they do today.

Certainly, *leadership today is less about what is, and more about what ought to be*; less about management skills, and more about the dynamic implementing of a holistic vision for humanity; less the hard-nosed decisions of the tough-minded entrepreneur and more the self-surrender to a transformative vision for all; less the work of the warrior, and more the achievements of the wizard.[20] Leadership needs wisdom, contemplation, ability to summon the Spirit, imagination, and love. Is the emphasis on hope a soft issue in leadership? No more! It is a central component.

The leader of hope finds his or her meaning in life in leadership. Such a leader is a person of strong values, has awareness of others' giftedness and potential for growth, and supports a vision of society based on a desired future. A person of integrity with respect and love for others, the leader appreciates that leadership is a dynamic approach to life in which all together seek truth, share love, and serve the common good. Unifying, serving, and building up are focuses of a new consciousness of leadership. The best leaders have faith in themselves, in other people, and in God's vision of promise.

These leaders are pioneers of hope. "Hope is an attitude in action. It enables people to mobilize their healing and their achieving powers. It helps them to transcend the difficulties of today and envision the potentialities of tomorrow. Hope enables people to find the will and the way to aspire to greatness. Hope is testimony to the power of the human spirit."[21] However, hope implies activity and hard work, for it takes a lot of courage to be a leader of hope. "Augustine suggests that hope has two lovely daughters: anger at the way things are and courage to change them."[22] But hope helps us transcend our boundaries as we thirst for something beyond us. It draws all dimensions of a person to a new level, gives clarity of judgment on decision making, and establishes an exciting perspective on life. Leaders find their own meaning in that to which they dedicate themselves in hope.[23]

CHAPTER THREE

PROPHETICAL LEADERSHIP

EADERS of hope challenge followers to change the present in light of the future. This is a form of prophetical leadership. It is common to think that a prophet is a leader who tells the community what will be in the future. This is not so! The essential task of a prophet is to tell the community what ought to be in the present. A prophet deals with the future insofar as it shows the good or bad consequences of the community's present course of action.[1] We find the word "prophet," or its equivalent, in many cultures, with antecedents in seers, dreamers, diviners, and visionaries. Today, "prophets" generally refers to those unique spiritual leaders who had incomparable impact upon Hebrew society from the eighth to the fifth centuries BCE, and who can become models for contemporary leaders of hope.

1. HOW PROPHETS LEAD

Going all the way back to Abraham, many individuals were called prophets. There were well known prophets during the reigns of King David and his successors; there were many secondary prophets, some named and some unnamed; and there were several well-known prophetesses. The one thing they all had in common was they communicated to the people the values of God, the vision of a world in the plan of God. Some were priests, but most were not; some were enthusiastic about their call, and others hated it; some worked individually, but some notable prophets worked within a brotherhood similar to a monastic community; some were paid professionals, even official court-appointed advisers, but others were free voices, eventually becoming a third role in society alongside king and priest. Some were like the wizards, seers, and advisers found in many cultures.[2] However, eventually there appear individuals of exceptional moral qualities—lonely, incorruptible leaders who were independent of society's power players in government, business, and religion. They had the moral courage to do what was right no matter what the consequences, risking reputation, opposition, and rejection.

The period of prophets that gives insight into contemporary prophetical leadership begins with Amos (c. 750 BCE) and Hosea (c. 745 BCE) and ends with Joel (c. 400 BCE). We can divide these singular individuals into three groups, each with a specific message for changed circumstances. Prior to the great Babylonian exile, when Palestine was a corridor for invasion, and its leaders made treaties with whoever would protect them, and when society evidenced decadence, religious corruption, and widespread injustice, seven great prophets arose to denounce injustice, oppression of the poor, lack of religious integrity, and disregard of the values of God's vision for humanity. These prophets, including the great figures Isaiah and Jeremiah, spoke out concerning what ought to be the values of their contemporary society.

With the exile to Babylon, the state was crushed, the nation shattered, the religious cult at an end, and the people overwhelmed by despair. In such changed circumstances, three powerful leaders emerged to give consolation, encouragement, and renewed confidence to an oppressed nation. With the exiles' return to Israel in the sixth century (c. 538 BCE), a further situation arose and a new group of six or seven prophets faced a different challenge in their leadership. Now the people needed to build a new community, and these prophets challenged the people to rebuild the city and temple, to reestablish authentic religious life, to take the opportunity to purify the moral and religious failures of the past, and to look forward with hope to a new age.

Prophetical leaders speak out of spiritual conviction and communicate to others the vision of God's will for contemporary society. They may denounce injustice, encourage and console people when they are oppressed, or challenge hopeful rebuilding—whatever seems appropriate to the current situation. These reactions are consistently faithful to the vision of God. A prophetical leader is a leader of hope who interacts with the present in light of the future to which God calls. Prophetical leadership is a form of spiritual leadership; it cuts through the failures of political, religious, or business groups, whenever they betray the people, and it demands change from all who fail to live the values to which humanity feels called. Prophetical leaders understand that leadership deals with big, global challenges, not simply running an organization. Leaders are social architects, influencing major issues affecting society.

These prophets, who give wonderful insights into leadership, had personal faith and knowledge of God's vision of promise and were filled with hope in its eventual implementation. While some were enthusiastic, and others oppressed by the task before them, they felt called to proclaim this message locally, even though they knew it would have wide-ranging impact. They were intensely aware that it was God's word they proclaimed and not their own, and that they must stand for these values whether people listened or not. Some became lonely individuals for their standards were too high; some were discouraged, ridiculed, rejected, and even completely broken by the people's unwillingness to listen. However, they knew this task was their destiny, and they plodded on with obedience to the call they felt, with spiritual perception of the vision of God, and with the ongoing conversion that sustained their fidelity to this hope.

The message of the prophets is always in keeping with the vision of hope. It has moral worth and immediate relevance—people know it is right whether they like it or not. Some prophets have great insight into political realities; others analyze the failures of organized religion; and all confront the abuse of power and people's infidelity to the values of God. These figures from centuries ago dealt with topics that are relevant today. To mention a few: Amos spoke of war crimes, injustice of social and political structures, decadent lifestyles, and unchecked exploitation of others. Hosea denounced general corruption, government leaders who ruin the nation, the folly of some foreign treaties, and political conspiracy. Micah addressed inequalities of the political-social set-up, tyranny by the wealthy, oppression by government, and sinful social structures. Each prophet's message could have been written to challenge our current social, political, business, and religious situations. To suggest prophets speak about the future that will be is to take the heart out of their message. They call their people to live the way they ought to live as part of God's vision for humanity. They are spiritual leaders who pass on to others what they know of God's vision for humanity. They make known to their people what they do not appreciate, have forgotten, or never knew. They convey their message primarily by words, sometimes by symbolic actions, and often by the example of their lives.

They see what others do not see. Rather than foretell, they forthtell; proclaiming in season and out of season the values that ought to guide humanity in daily life. They have a vision of the unity of humanity, built on fidelity to God's vision; they urge its implementation and denounce infidelity. Prophets like Amos insist on a spirit of community and condemn power structures that support exaggerated lifestyles for the wealthy in their palatial homes, summer homes here and there, and sumptuous feasting, while the poor are exploited, practically sold into slavery, all with the knowledge of a corrupt judicial system. Hosea insists that sexual infidelity and abuse point to infidelity to the values of God. Jeremiah calls for a whole new vision of life, a new set of values based on the spirit of God. He says laws must be written on men's, and women's hearts, not remain an immature external obligation, but become an intimate part of life. Isaiah is the original source of servant leadership, Ezekiel calls for group action in the work of justice. Jeremiah and Malachi speak out against unjust wages, several against fraud, others against the unfairness of the judicial system. Jeremiah speaks against those who refuse to free slaves, Amos against the injustices of the banking system, and Isaiah against tyrannical lawmakers who write laws for their own gain. Many denounce those who grind the faces of the poor into the ground, and both Isaiah and Jeremiah criticize irresponsible leaders whether civic or religious. Several call for a new covenantal relationship among men and women and with God.[3]

Prophets describe what ought to be the values of humanity in politics, social interactions, organized religion, legal matters, and business practice. They bring the leadership insights to bear on very practical issues and constantly insist what ought to be the values of a people who wish to live in faith and hope. Jeremiah and Isaiah insist on justice: "Execute justice in the morning, and deliver from the hand of the oppressor anyone who has been robbed, or else my wrath will go forth like fire, and burn, with no one to quench it, because of your evil doings." "Learn to do good; seek justice, rescue the oppressed, defend the orphan, plead for the widow." Amos cries out against corruption and greed: "They hate the one who reproves in the gate, and they abhor the one who speaks the truth. Therefore because you trample on the poor and take from them levies of grain, you have built houses of hewn stone, but you shall not live in them; you have planted pleasant vineyards, but you shall not drink their wine. For I know how many are your transgressions, and how great are your sins—you who afflict the righteous, who take a bribe, and push aside the needy in the gate." Third Isaiah consoles his people and urges them to rebuild their society on the foundations of justice: "If you offer your food to the hungry and satisfy the needs of the afflicted, then your light shall rise in the darkness and your gloom be like the noonday."[4] Jeremiah pleads for honesty and integrity: "But your eyes and heart are only on your dishonest gain, for shedding innocent blood, and for practicing oppression and violence."

Third Isaiah links religious devotion to justice; "Is not this the fast that I choose: to loose the bonds of injustice, to undo the thongs of the yoke, to let the oppressed go free, and to break every yoke? Is it not to share your bread with the hungry, and bring the homeless poor into your house; when you see the naked, to cover them, and not to hide yourself from your own kin?"[5]

Jeremiah, Amos, and others condemn religion that is not connected with social justice or is irrelevant to daily life. "Do not trust in these deceptive words: 'This is the temple of the LORD, the temple of the LORD, the temple of the LORD.' For [I will accept you only] if you truly amend your ways and your doings, if you truly act justly one with another, if you do not oppress the alien, the orphan, and the widow, or shed innocent blood in this place." Amos claims that some cannot wait for the religious feasts to finish so that they can get back to their cheating and extortion: "When will the new moon be over so that we may sell grain; and the Sabbath, so that we may offer wheat for sale? We will make the ephah small and the shekel great, and practice deceit with false balances." Isaiah says God turns away from inauthentic religion: "When you stretch out your hands, I will hide my eyes from you; even though you make many prayers, I will not listen; your hands are full of blood." Micah sums up the crucial insight of prophetical leadership's message concerning what should guide our lives: "What does the LORD require of you but to do justice, and to love kindness, and to walk humbly with your God?"[6] So the prophets denounce current ways of living that violate God's vision for humanity. They demand action in the present in light of the future. They are leaders of hope.

2. CONTEMPORARY PROPHETICAL LEADERSHIP

We can complement our reflection on the lives and common message of the great prophetical leaders of old with awareness that Christ too was a model of prophetical leadership.[7] Leading figures in the early church continued this emphasis on prophetical leadership.[8] The Second Vatican Council picked up this theme and insisted that prophetical leadership continues today. "Christ, the great Prophet, who proclaimed the kingdom of His Father by the testimony of His life and by the power of His words, continually fulfills His prophetic office until His full glory is revealed."[9]

Two convictions characterize prophetical leaders: the integrity of the message and their absolute awareness that it is their destiny to proclaim and embody it for others. Contemporary prophetical leaders know that they are, and must be, intimately connected with the institution they serve, but they are also called, are set apart, and must be faithful to God's values whatever the personal costs. While they feel called, they are not born to be prophetical leaders. Most make themselves into the leaders they become. "Before they become prophets, they were of the stuff from which prophets could be made."[10] Authentic leaders in contemporary society will be rejected, ridiculed by the pseudowise figures in government, society, business, health care, and religion, who will always insist the prophet's message is ideal, naïve, and unreal, and that the prophets should not meddle or rock the boat. However, the prophet feels compelled to insist on the purity of the message, for as Amos said, when the Lord calls, who can refuse to accept the task of prophetical leadership (Amos 3:8)?

Prophetical leaders must be made of the right stuff, for there is so much money, greed, power, sex, and control in modern society that these temptations overwhelm leaders in all walks of life. In presenting a vision of the common good, prophetical leaders must not only be inspired but also inspire others with conviction that a new spirit of human interaction is possible—their message rings with freshness, integrity, power, and hope. They must stay the course whatever the cost.

Prophetical leaders are marginal, not part of the mainstream of managerial leadership. Many people will find their bold message too controversial for contemporary organizational life. Unfortunately we have become too accustomed to things as they are and have been, and we need courage to risk something different. But the purpose of prophetical leadership is more radical than social change, for it is part of an integrated vision of humanity's covenant with God. Prophetical leaders show the people God's future for them. "The task of prophetic imagination and ministry is to bring to public expression those very hopes and yearnings that have been denied so long and suppressed so deeply that we no longer know they are there."[11]

These hopes and yearnings grow out of the present; they form the vision for which we long. Prophetical leadership brings the future vision of hope to bear on concrete contemporary decision making. Vision is really a verb, not a noun; it refers to the daily attitude of living each moment in the future vision. It requires courage, ethics, and covenantal thinking; it is the motivation to move beyond the present society with its local business or organizational thinking, beyond the corporate shared visions that are frequently based on the lowest common denominator, to a social and community vision. So much of contemporary society is no longer worth propping up, and a prophetical leader offers an alternative form of social life, based on a vision of God's plan for the world. All life, including organizational life, must reflect the values of the covenant. Prophetical leaders are always seekers after what is best for all the people they serve, and they are visionaries of how things should be.[12]

A prophetical leader must turn the vision of hope into practical involvement. Vision is always a mere dream unless it is implemented.[13] The prophet's compelling vision must include dedicated service; in other words, a sense of mission lived in values. The values do not create the vision, but they measure the rightness of the vision. If the prophet can enthusiastically persuade others to pursue the vision of hope, the vision will attract commitment, energize followers, create meaning in workers' lives, establish standards of excellence, and bridge the gap between the present and the future.[14] This results in a shared purpose, and when the prophetical leader then empowers others, makes appropriate organizational changes, and introduces strategic thinking to attain the vision, then there emerges successful visionary leadership.[15] Such prophetical leadership persuades others, fosters participation, and responds to the deepest yearnings of good people.

Prophetical leaders do not own the vision; they present hopes in relation to the final vision, they "see in a mirror dimly" (1 Cor 13:12). When they think they do own the vision, they become autocratic, imposing their views on others. The vision is based on God's hope and promise; it is always evolving as people and circumstances change; it can never be so exalted that it is unconnected with people's lives; and it is always a little fuzzy and in need of ongoing clarification. After all, everyone has hopes and dreams. There are existing spiritual resources of the organization, and the prophetical leader brings them together to enrich the initial vision. The prophetical leader must be willing to let go of his or her interpretation of aspects of the vision so that it can become the group's vision. These leaders continually follow an evolving vision rather than leading with one of their own.

Prophetical leadership is proactive, as leaders ask what it is that needs to be done. They present a liberating vision of hope that when others see it, they recognize it as what they hope for. The leader's task is then to develop shared commitment to this compelling vision and institutionalize it in the organization's values. The vision of a desirable and attainable future gives alternatives, different choices, and new creative strategies. It is specific but open to further specification by the group.[16]

The prophetical leader sees the larger picture and presents a context for understanding organizational life. The vision is radical but also part of a tradition of God's vision of hope; so it is radical, but well known. The prophetical leader can often experience total rejection, but strives for responsiveness in the hearers. The leader must focus, challenge, and liberate, and eventually must generate the needed trust to encourage others to change the organizational culture. So the skilled and courageous prophetical leader pushes people to satisfy their own yearnings, as they see that the vision embodies their dreams in action.

The prophet accepts the drudgery of leadership. He or she must work to make the community powerful in attaining its vision. There is no vision when people feel powerless or hopeless. Many years ago, "We discovered that the effective leader seemed able to create a vision that gave workers the feeling of being at the active centers of the social order."[17] This implies all the usual skills of leadership, collaboration, empowerment, team building, and ongoing assessment. The vision—since it is the vision of promise—has the inherent power to draw others to its goals, but there are many obstacles in the way.[18] In fact, there has been a lot of disillusionment with leaders and leadership, creating an antipathy that prophetical leaders will have to face. Disillusionment preceded the encouraging developments in transformational leadership. However, we are back into a further period of disillusionment with leadership from which perhaps the leader of hope can yet redeem us.

3. TEN TASKS OF PROPHETICAL LEADERS

1. Do More

Development in leadership theory and practice has been outstanding in the last quarter century. However, they have not produced a batch of outstanding leaders who have had an impact on organizational life. There comes a time when even the good that has been achieved is simply not enough. We need leaders who are willing to do more, stand for more, be more, and yes, even suffer more in order to achieve more. The greedy, the controllers, the abusers, the power hungry still seem to determine the direction of organizational life. Leaders of hope must become prophetical leaders who will present to society what ought to be done to have just organizational and professional lives. We have already considered the concept of *magis*, "the more," that leads beyond professional commitment to discretionary commitment that is the singular requirement for great change. We need prophetical leaders with generous hearts who will give their all to enable organizations and help society achieve their ends in the vision of God.

2. *Live with Urgency and Patience*

Both qualities are needed together. It is urgent that leaders of hope insist on implementing the vision of promise, but it will take a lot of patient collaboration to achieve it. We have presumed for too long that leaders in business, health care, politics, and religion know what they are doing, that they have agendas that will improve life, and that we can leave them in charge; they might even say they act in God's name.[19] No! Absolutely not so! It is urgent that we insist on different values, skills, and vision in those who preside over organizational life. Among the prophetical leader's tasks is to redefine what it means to be a leader, to become captive to urgent change, to insist on what needs to be done today that was not done yesterday. Leaders of the past have rarely attained the hope and promise we have placed in them, but it is not too late for new leaders of hope to implement new possibilities in human interactions and organizational life.

3. *Be Authentic*

Leadership today is a new form of prophecy. The leader of hope reminds us about what it is we believe in and hope for. The prophetical leader is not about improving his or her own lot but about interpreting and implementing a vision. The prophetical leader knows that everything must reflect the vision. The intensity of the prophet's conviction has to be matched by followers' conviction that the propheti-

44

cal leader will never swerve from the purity of the message, all decisions will be made in light of the vision, personal life will always reflect it, and the vision will always reverberate in everything that is done. Prophetical leadership is not only action done with integrity, but also the attitude of never being satisfied with some reduced or partial realization of the vision. Followers trust that the leader will always be authentic, and that hopes will become values in action.

4. Confront Injustice

A prophetical leader bears the burdens of the oppressed and challenges the injustices of oppressive individuals and structures. Like the prophets of old, the prophetical leader feels impelled to denounce injustices wherever discovered. Our world is steeped in injustice, much of it so rooted in the subconscious of our culture that it has become the normal order of the day. The prophetical leader will develop goals and strategies to uproot injustice. The prophetical leader is always a part of an organization and so plays a role in its development and financial stability. Confronting injustice requires prudence, patience, and firm determination to take whatever opportunities occur. A prophetical leader will focus on attitudes to workers: respect, just wages, dignity, responsibilities, and working environment. He or she will give due care to structures: collaboration, team building, decision making, due process, and collegial administration. A prophet will insist that values play a major role: basic values, ethics, mission, vision, and goal setting. The leader will also focus everyone's concern on customers and subcontractors: just treatment, product quality, safety, fair value, and service. Justice needs to be part of the system, and wise leaders will gradually transform their organizations to portray values that are part of a vision of promise.

5. *Lead with Courage*

Courage is born of the conviction that one stands for the right values. As one doubts this, courage wanes. The prophetical leader has a deep sense of the meaning of life and how that impacts individuals. The fact that all this is part of God's vision of promise intensifies a feeling of hopefulness that in turn strengthens courage. The prophets of old "made great demands, had courageous words of discernment and constructive criticism for the bearers of authority in church, state and society," and modern prophetical leaders can do no less.[20] Of course, leading with courage will require resilience, as the leader faces obstacles, opposition, and even hatred from those who lose when structures change. The prophetical leader must denounce the world of the powerful, elite, and dominant, and confront the world of despair of the oppressed. People do not want their lives decided by ignorant, incompetent, wealthy individuals who buy their way into power, or by individuals chosen by ideological nepotism. The prophetical leader will need three forms of courage: "the courage to see and speak the truth, the courage to create and affirm a vision of the desired state, and the courage to persevere, to hold the course."[21]

6. *Create Dangerously*

Prophetical leaders must do more than master the basic routines of leadership. They must create dangerously—insisting on what needs to be done to be faithful to the vision of promise.[22] This means an ability to reshape the future that people can expect in organizations, and to do this in spite of the lurking dangers from people who want to preserve the past or from those who know no better than clinging to positions. The prophetical leader is a catalyst for change, a herald of new approaches to people within organizations, a seer of what could be, a revealer of justice, a proclaimer of authentic community life.[23] Being creative in implementing a desired and hoped-for future is a dangerous task, and often the selfishly powerful will do all in their power to domesticate the leader's dangerous hopes. But the prophetical leader's efforts to create dangerously are ethically sound alternatives that can redeem organizations from their sins and embrace a vision of hope for leadership and organizational life. Prophetical leaders give us direction through uncharted opportunities.

7. Savor Suffering

Prophetical leadership implies suffering. Jesus said, "I tell you solemnly no prophet is ever accepted in his own country" (Luke 4:24). Every day the prophetical leader will say, "This situation is breaking my heart." However, he or she must go on, naming the pain and accepting it as part of the transformation of community. Prophetical leaders must live with rejection, random pain, and uncertainty. More than anything else, the leader must live with the pain of others who have no voice, who face rejection, abuse, neglect, and hopelessness. A key feature of the prophet is compassion—suffering with others. "Quite clearly, the one thing the dominant culture cannot tolerate or co-opt is compassion, the ability to stand in solidarity with the victims of the present order."[24] The prophetical leader lives in solidarity with those who suffer, listens to their stories and gets a feel for how they feel, and tries to view everything from the perspective of those who suffer. "Suffering made audible and visible produces hope, articulated grief is the gate of newness, and the history of Jesus is the history of entering into the pain and giving it voice."[25] The prophetical leader will grapple with suffering, grieve and share the anguish of those who are oppressed, and then focus his or her strategies on how to transform society into what it should be.

8. Contemplate the Vision

The prophet is a witness to the word he or she proclaims. The prophet can only speak to others with conviction and persuasion when a certain depth in appreciating the vision has been reached. This means contemplating the vision and values of God. This is done in quiet time, in reflection, and in prayer. It means emptying oneself and opening oneself to be filled by God. A spirit of poverty and emptiness, followed by attentive listening with one's heart and mind, can lead to prophetic insight. Vision is the art of seeing what others do not yet see or maybe do not yet want to see. It is acquired most particularly in prayer, in the encounter with the God of promise, and it is here that the leader finds solutions to problems and new directions for personal and organizational life.

9. *Establish an Alternative Consciousness*

The essential task of a prophet is to denounce what is when it is unjust and to proclaim what ought to be. When the current situation is acceptable, there is no need for a prophet. When the present situation falls short of the ideal, a crisis follows that calls forth the response of leadership. Then the prophet experiences a call. Essentially the prophet presents an alternative consciousness, telling us that society must be, and can be, different. When we look at business, health care, politics, and religion, each has images that they believe are the only acceptable approaches to their organizations. For the most part, they are all wrong! In the last decade we have witnessed overwhelming disasters of failed leadership.[26] All aspects of social life are in a mess, followers have reduced respect—if any at all—for their so-called leaders, and followers find that over and over again they are ignored. "The task of prophetic ministry is to nurture, nourish, and evoke a consciousness and perception alternative to the consciousness and perception of the dominant culture around us."[27] This implies dismantling the values of the dominant culture, providing alternatives for people to live by, and introducing new relationships within community. This is painful and costly work; it is the contemporary prophetical leader's bearing of the cross.[28] For the community, it will demand

48

patience, mutual respect, and mutual dependence. Eventually the community becomes a prophetical community as it lives out the vision of hope. People want to participate, not to be managed.

10. Teach a New Perspective on Leadership without Power

Jesus came in the form of a servant and insisted on servant leadership among his own followers. He gives an alternative form of administration and government that is not rooted in power. Approaches based on oppressive power must be uprooted. It is not possible to construct servant leadership on the typical foundations we find in contemporary organizational life. The Christian Scriptures present Mary as an example of the humility of the servant who responds to God's call. "Forgotten are her prophetic words about how God 'scattered the proud...put down the mighty...exalted those of low degree...filled the hungry...and the rich has sent empty away.'"[29] Servant leadership is revolutionary. Prophetical leaders are men and women of humility, selfless in service, loving toward others. The prophet knows how much he or she needs others; he or she transfers power, responsibility, and accountability to workers at all levels; works for synergy to capitalize on the gifts of all; and appreciates that leadership can surface at any point in the organization. Prophetical leaders establish organizations where government is collegial, mission and values guide the direction, administration is collaborative, decisions are made at the lowest possible level in the organization, teams are self-managed, community is continually fostered, workers are appreciated, the culture is one of openness and trust, and all share in ongoing education.[30]

CHAPTER FOUR

THE TRANSCENDENT
IN LEADERSHIP

W E saw in the last chapter that the prophetical leader communicates to others how things ought to be; he or she proclaims the values of God's plan for the world. On the other hand, the mystical leader—one who appreciates the transcendent in leadership—communicates to others the personal experience of the values of God's vision of promise. Mystical leadership refers to leadership that results from a profound spiritual experience. In this chapter we deal with the roots of leadership in a personal transforming experience that is a mystical journey.

We tend to associate mystical experiences with an isolated, intensive, meditative type of personality, which is not necessarily so. Many everyday mystics are very busy, involved, and productive organizational leaders. The idea that mystics are the ones who are always getting in trouble with the organization is not true; often they are the ones who transform an organization. Nowadays there is a worldwide mystical awakening among many people and professions. Great leaders in all walks of life are becoming mystics and appreciate the values of mystical leadership. Their vision, skills, attitudes, and behaviors will be different than those of other leaders because they are moved by a profound insight and an experience of how things can be different. They have experience of hope. Nowadays we see new paradigms in science and organizational life: process over substance, interdependence over independence, participation over objectivity, collaboration over hierarchy, and so on. The focus is always on what results from experience; the new paradigm is based on a mystical consciousness.

Mystical leaders must still get the job done, be productive, meet goals, and earn profits. They might have a different vision of leadership, but they still earn the financial margins and achieve the needed organizational change. Many will undoubtedly say this is not possible. However, we have already seen very profitable organizations based on values—organizations that are socially responsible, green, employee owned, and owned by women—and they have all worked well. The mystical leader is as competent as any other leader, or maybe more so. But this leader is a person of interiority and hope, and builds interactions exclusively on what he or she has experienced of justice, compassion, respect, community, mutuality, and love. This leadership is built on the experience of the vision of promise.[1] Mystical leaders are leaders of hope, for they have experienced the hope-filled vision to which they dedicate their lives.

1. THE LEADER'S MYSTICAL JOURNEY

Leadership theorists have presented us with several stages in leadership, in a leader's interactions with goals, followers, or changing situations, and in followers' responses to their leaders. All these ideas are worthy of consideration and can clarify development of leadership skills. However, on the more important level of human maturity and spiritual growth, there are two essential stages in a leader's personal development, separated from each other by one of the most profound spiritual experiences of life. To appreciate that "the heart of all leadership is in a leader's heart" calls the leader-to-be to make "an uncommon journey of spirit."[2] However, this journey is more than discovering the best that lies within us; it is an experience of the parallel roles of spirituality and leadership. It is a journey from what is natural to what is above our natural responses; from an ascetical focus like the training of an athlete to the mystical focus on values beyond the normal horizons of life; from a meditative, discursive approach when one thinks things through to a contemplative, intuitive approach when one gains insights into the realities of life; from an exclusively active approach to one's leadership to an emphasis on the value of receptivity in one's life and growth.

These two stages in leadership are good, and both are found in very fine leaders. They are beyond the preliminary training needed to initiate a person to leadership. In fact, even stage one requires its own dedicated preparation in study, practice, behavior, and research. However, most leaders spend all their lives in the first stage, do not have the courage to go further, know no better, and will never change. They work with dedicated and patient endurance unenlightened by hope, and grounded in what can only be seen by the eyes. I prefer to refer to these dedicated people as inspired managers, since what they do affects primarily the organization and not its people. A few leaders move to the second stage, and they are mystical leaders. Their work transforms not only the organization but also each of its members, individually and as a community.

In the first stage, an inspired manager acts as if everything depends on him or her. This kind of leader fills his or her every minute with effort, planning, programming, strategizing, and evaluating. The leader at this stage emphasizes his or her strengths, knowledge, and learning, and is very much in control of self. The second stage contrasts with this. The leader in stage two reflects on life values as a source for a different kind of leadership. He or she treasures quiet time and an effortless approach to life. The leader accepts his or her own weakness and values unknowing and unlearning, convinced of benefiting from being controlled by a greater power than self. The former stresses doing, the latter being. The former looks with the eyes of experience, the latter with the eyes of faith and hope. The former reasons; the latter values intuition. The former is centered on self, the latter on transcendent values beyond self. The former is mainly reactive, the latter proactive. If leaders in both stages are wise and attentive, then the first will have an opportunity to purify false values, but the latter will receive an illumination concerning leadership and the vision of promise that comes from no source other than contemplation and self-immersion in the values of God.

Leaders in stage one strive to be good at their jobs; they search every way to be better; they do not waste time; and they avoid silence and emptiness. They benefit from getting rid of false values and learn a lot from the memory of others' experiences and successes. They are often a little compulsive in their approach to leadership and tend to view it narrowly. Leaders who have moved to stage two have developed a facility in letting go and receiving from outside self. They can surrender themselves to greater values and enter silence with awareness of their own emptiness. They learn from focusing not on the past but on the vision of hope in the future. They are leaders of compassion and empathetic listening and tend to view leadership broadly.

The leader in stage one uses task-oriented, instrumental, and relational skills, carefully sets goals and objectives, listens to what is said, comes up with good answers to problems, and sees service of others as a major technique in leadership. The leader in stage two uses imaginative, contemplative, and system skills, recognizes that goals and objectives are to be found in the vision of promise, comes up with good questions that will need to be addressed, listens to what is not said, draws out the feelings and concerns of others, and sees service of others as a personal vocation. In the first stage the leader is always moving forward to the attaining of values under the pressure of outside forces. In the latter stage he or she feels drawn to values beyond self, and discovers "the well-spring of real learning is aspiration, imagination, and experimentation."[3]

These two stages in human maturity and spiritual growth form the basis for a leader's spiritual development. They are closely linked together. The active effort-filled stage is necessary for everyone and always precedes the contemplative and receptive experiences of stage two. Stage two includes two focuses: first, a moving forward to new experiences, a sense of being drawn to immerse oneself in the vision of promise with characteristics we have just seen; second, a refocusing on stage one but with the attitudes of stage two. The mystical leader does not neglect the basic leadership values and skills of stage one but transforms them with the aid of a new awareness that comes in the mystical encounter with God, God's vision and call, and the specific values of the vision of promise. For the mystical leader, the new awareness of stage two is not a substitute for stage one, but is stage one transferred to a new level. A leader who goes to stage two feels the need to repair the past. "New ways of thinking about familiar things can release new energies and make all manner of things possible."[4]

So stage one always precedes stage two. The latter never happens except following a profound spiritual, conversional experience in which one is drawn to live for the values of God's vision of promise. Stage two not only moves forward in hope to new horizons but also moves back to retransform the foundational non-selfish aspects of stage one. These are two different horizons of leadership, two different rhythms of a leader's personality, two ways of personalizing one's life and leadership.

Mystical leaders are men and women of presence who bring a new meaning to work, to relationships, to ethics and justice, to institutional purpose and mission. Their leadership builds on insight, intuition, artistic creativity, poetry, friendship, and community. They not only treasure what can be measured but also the untapped resources of transcendent values. For them, spirituality is an intimate part of leadership excellence. They are men and women of wisdom, a little like the wizards of old. "Wizards bring imagination, insight, creativity, vision and meaning, and magic to the work of leadership."[5]

Mystical leaders are marginal like prophets are, but whereas the prophet emphasizes the power of the word, the mystic emphasizes the power of love. However, the love that motivates the mystical leader is also a transforming power, as is the word of the prophetical leader. One writer refers to six landscapes of love—as desire, feelings, action, giving, energy, and Spirit—and he describes these as wanting love, emotional love, doing love, selfless love, powered love, and being love.[6] Mystical leadership is the result of a contemplative experience of God and of God's vision of promise.[7] A leader can deepen this experience by reflection on creation (*via positiva*),[8] by letting go and letting be (*via negativa*), in breakthrough and giving birth to self and God (*via creativa*), and by way of compassion and social justice (*via transformativa*). These four traditional focuses of Christian contemplative and mystical tradition emphasize appreciation, detachment, creativity, and compassion.[9] The four facets of love form the daily commitment of the mystical leader, and it is the call of love that gives hope.

2. THE DARKNESS OF LEADERSHIP

The transition from stage one to stage two is painful for a leader. It is a crisis of confidence in what the leader has so far been doing; it is a sense of loss that former successes no longer mean anything; it is the death of past values and the willingness to let them die for they are based on a vision that is too small. The leader who goes through this spiritual experience of passage from a set of old values to a set of new values feels the ground beneath giving way. The leader grasps that there is more to life than meeting goals and objectives, increasing profits, satisfying shareholders, marketing a successful product or service. People, community, justice, others' fulfillment, love, and changing the values of society are all more important. All good leaders achieve the former; mystical leaders also achieve the latter, and so are filled with hope.

The transition is a painful conversion, but we desperately need people willing to endure it and participate in the transformation. Leadership must change! We cannot continue with the innumerable failures of recent years. Leaders in business, politics, and religion have become arrogant beyond their predecessors. We have witnessed a decline in democracy and a maintenance of myths of leadership that have led people to despise their own leaders. Were people to have a say in choosing their own leaders in business, politics, or religion, very few of current officeholders would survive the first round of selection. Leaders must change, or organizations should be left to die. The ashes of previous leadership styles are in the grate, and there is no phoenix to emerge.

The transition through which a good leader passes in becoming a mystical leader is a dark night. This term, "dark night," comes from the poetry and commentaries of the Spanish Christian mystic John of the Cross, who was also a dynamic and multitalented organizational leader. The dark night is a stage in spiritual life when one begins to see things in a different way than one ever has before. Sometimes a person cannot see because everything around is dark, but on other occasions a person cannot see because of the brightness of illumination—like standing in the headlights of an oncoming car. "Dark night" for John is the latter experience, and so he refers to this transition as a dark night, a glad night, a guiding night, a night more lovely than the dawn, a transforming night, a night of union and love.[10] For a leader this night can be an illumination of the direction of authentic leadership.

The transition to a new level of leadership is an experience of darkness that enables the leader to stop seeing in one way and to start seeing things in a new way. The experience itself is a form of contemplation. Contemplation requires stillness and a quiet waiting for values beyond ourselves. It comes to a person who is comfortable with self, not afraid to be alone, has a clear sense of purpose and vocation, appreciates beauty in all aspects of life, spends time in reflection, welcomes emptiness, takes care of one's body, and nourishes self with education.[11] It requires an ability to be still, to be inspired, to concentrate, and to be silent.

Contemplation is essentially a form of wordless reflection or prayer in which a person ceases to be active and becomes passive and receptive, open to receive from God, and called to a new vocation to leadership. It is preceded by a period of purification in which all that one valued is shown and experienced to be insignificant in relation to what could be. We feel called to stop learning in the ways we have learned and to stop knowing in the ways we have known. This is part of doing away with the idols of organizational life, of getting rid of the gods of prior visions of leadership. So much leadership and so many organizations are diseased, and we must burn away the sin and selfishness before real healing can take place. In this contemplative transition we begin to listen to a different voice. We discover that leadership is not what we thought it was; that leaders do not act in the way we thought they should; that good followers do not react in the ways we thought they would.

These experiences at first shock us, leave us discouraged, and give us a sense of failure in having spent life dedicated to the wrong values. It means recognizing and addressing our counterfeit selves. Along with the shock goes an underlying fear—fear to face the unknown, fear to face the wholeness of God's gifts. It is part of the process of entering the darkness of leadership, an experience in which one feels emptied of former success, competence, skills, and vision. A leader must savor the pain of this loss and become convinced in the depths of soul that former values are inadequate. As the leader wrestles with the contradictions of life, he or she must feel the pain of this loss in order to emerge into a new life where all former weaknesses are transformed. However, only when one is emptied of false values can one be filled with new ones. For we as Christian believers it is God who draws us to a new way of life, fills us with the new values of the vision of promise, and sets us on a new direction in leadership.

The mystical experience is not reserved for monks or nuns. Provided he or she can maintain a little reflection amid a busy life, or not be completely distracted, that leader can open self to the transforming experience of mystical encounter with God and values beyond the normal horizons of life. "The transformational leader is an experienced mediator. He [or she] can enter the silence, wherever he [or she] is and whatever he [or she] is doing. By learning to span consciousness, part of his [or her] awareness is always centered in the inner temple while the remainder of his [or her] consciousness is focused upon the task at hand."[12] This is a breakthrough experience, an immersion in a mystery beyond us, and it leads to clarity of vision, insightful responsiveness to the vision of promise, an expansion of the mind's perception, and insight into the realities of leadership and organizational life. It is a new knowledge. "The task of leadership requires the courage of conviction to venture beyond our comfort zone of existing knowledge and experience to discover new and alternative ways of thinking, acting, and behaving to lift our organizations and ourselves to greater levels of accomplishment."[13] It is more than a new knowledge. "A new kind of spiriting is afoot these days....individuals will be called to face beyond within themselves—without a priest, without a church, without ceremonies—simply within their own nature, all alone."[14]

The transitional experience also brings peace, comfort, a healthy indifference, and hope. The leader no longer fears failure, since success comes from outside self. He or she can now make conscious choices for new values, rearrange elements to construct new possibilities, envision structures never before tried, use criteria unheard of previously, give rein to the fruits of imagination—all part of learning how to learn, learning how to hope, and learning how to love. The leader is alone in this experience, but it is the occasion of self-discovery and the answer to one's search for meaning in life. This transition is a letting go of the past and a purification of the arrogance, greed, and selfishness that taint leadership. However, it is also a rededication to seek the best whatever the cost, to pursue what is the most loving thing to do. One becomes one's true self in the contemplative experience; one sees one's deepest needs and challenges. In the experience an individual gains a clear picture of the direction life and leadership should take. It is a simple, intuitive, and immediate experience that manifests the obvious way things should be, and it bears no disagreement; it is the vision of promise and hope.

3. BEYOND NORMAL HORIZONS

1. Learning a New Way to Be a Leader

Those who have the courage to make the transition to a new vision of leadership stretch their awareness and consciousness. In their meditation and prayer they encounter the living God, challenging them to be faithful to a new vision of leadership. They will still experience traces of the confusion, discouragement, disturbance, and even depression of the transition period, but they will now have new energy, courage, and enthusiasm for the clarified vocation they feel. Participation in the creativity of the new vision of leadership helps them break through the ring of limitation that formerly surrounded them. In the contemplative, mystical experience they know their own truth and calling. This experience is essentially an experience of God's values for the human community. It is not only that the leader learns a new way of being a leader, but that the leader experiences those qualities that constitute the new leadership to which he or she is called. Values emerge in contemplation—the leader experiences justice, love, community, mercy, forgiveness, and so on, all gifts of God within the prayerful experience. The leader is put in contact with the vision and feels called to pass it on to others. The spiritual encounter is an anticipated experience of what we hope for.

2. Appreciating One's Role in the World

One of the immediate results of this transformation is that the leader enjoys a quieter life. He or she feels confirmed in peace and tranquility. While having seen one's own dark areas of life, the leader is now reconciled to a future in hope. He or she is now centered and inner directed. The leader becomes an ordinary, everyday mystic.

Seeing life more immediately and objectively the leader can also live more peacefully with problems of organizations. In this experience an individual gains a new self-concept. First one can appreciate one's own weakness and the fact that one is a wounded leader in need of a new direction and in need of others. It is a time to discover one's true self, to care for oneself in a new way, to see one's own giftedness and others' giftedness too in the plan of God. The leader identifies self in a new way, as called to the courage of hope and as dedicated to be a channel of leadership to others. The contemplative, mystical experience is an immediate, intuitive encounter with reality. One sees oneself exactly as one is, with one's failings and strengths. The mystical encounter is an opportunity for personal enrichment like no other.

3. Accepting Leadership as a Personal Vocation

A leader becomes enthralled by the beauty of the vision of leadership and drawn to implement it. He or she lives with a new perspective on life. Most leaders can answer the question "how should something be done?" but the mystical leader can answer "why should something be done?" The leader's new vocation includes overcoming boundaries and seeing an integrated vision of the whole, appreciating differences, and stressing community and love. The leader sees that real learning comes in contemplation, and he or she is enriched by gifts of clarity, perspective, penetration, and connectivity. Finally, as part of the new perspective, the leader perceives an expansive understanding of his or her leadership and appreciates how values learned for leadership can also enrich relationships, family, and friends. Following a contemplative, mystical experience a leader develops new priorities and acts differently because of a new awareness. The leader must continue to nourish life through reflection, but also feels called to value people, to treat everyone graciously, to foster reconciliation, to practice empathetic and transformational listening, and to spread love.

4. Occupying All One's Energy in Love

The goal of the spiritual journey of a leader is union with God's plan for the human community, a loving union with God and the leadership that God wills for humanity. The great mystic John of the Cross described his own feelings in this way: "Now I occupy my soul and all my energy in God's service....nor have I any other work now that my every act is love."[15] Mysticism now means that the leader understands that God now acts, hopes, loves, and serves through him or her. This transforming love enthuses the leader for life ahead and produces in the leader a disinterest for any other approach to leadership that is not focused on love for others. The skills remain, the attitudes are refocused, and the behaviors are refined, but above all there is a renewed sense of destiny. The purpose of one's life and leadership is to achieve good. Mystical leadership can never take the place of the total commitment to a skilled and visionary approach to one's organization, its people, its mission, and its future. Leadership is now grounded in a new knowledge of God and a new dedication to love-directed choices and decisions.

5. Living and Working for Community Growth

The more visible results of transformation in leadership include a positive, appreciative attitude to all who form part of the organization. Respect, sensitivity, openness, gratitude, compassion, and love will manifest themselves in more collaborative structures, opportunities for creativity, team building, allowing failure without reprimand, facilitating the best in each one, participation in decision making, and shared planning, vision, mission, and goal setting. All these are practical manifestations of the conviction concerning community, mutuality, and shared vocation that a leader experiences in a spiritual encounter. A leader will also want to invest in outreach to the wider community personally, through others, and by organizational involvement. An expansive view of the vocation to leadership implies that the transformation a leader can facilitate can never be restricted to his or her own business. A person who has entered the transformational experience will be a better spouse, parent, neighbor, citizen, and participant in the world community. These practical signs of human interdependence, needed care of the environment, and political responsibility all arise from experiencing the vision of how things should be.

6. Seeing the World with Its Goodness and Evil

The leader who has journeyed through transformation and entered the darkness of leadership can never be naïve. He or she has seen both good and bad, can always be hopeful, and knows that sin and evil are part of life that needs to be transformed. This kind of leader can always make the tough decisions since he or she knows they are necessary for authentic human values and community. However, the mystical leader can make tough decisions with understanding, compassion, and vision. To say you must be hard nosed, or that it is lonely at the top are comments of the incompetent who are themselves naïve in thinking their worldview is accurate. The leader of hope is committed to struggle for change that is in keeping with God's vision for all humanity.

7. Renewing One's Life and Leadership

The mystical leader is a leader of hope. He or she experiences the hope and then must give an account of the hope within. The intuitive experience is the basis of sudden and significant breakthroughs in one's leadership. It is an experience of enlightenment. I indicated that the goal of the spiritual journey of a leader is union with God and God's plan for humanity—what I have called the vision of hope or promise. However, this union itself leads to the transformation and integral renewal of the leader. These are two facets of the same reality—one does not happen without the other. Having endured the transitions and the darkness of leadership, a leader emerges with a new sense of self, a new confidence in the vocation of leadership, and an inability to do anything but serve others through leadership. A leader of hope is a prophetical leader and also a mystical leader. All other forms of leadership are shadowy preparations for what a person can become and what the world desperately needs.

CHAPTER FIVE

CHARISMATIC LEADERSHIP

NOW and again in leadership studies, as in other disciplines, scholars and practitioners take vocabulary that had a very precise original meaning and give it a new one that fits their theories and empirical analyses. There is nothing wrong with this approach; in fact, giving new meanings to old concepts is very common, even though the new one is not always an improvement on the old. We have already seen that the contemporary use of the term "prophetical leadership" is quite different than its original meaning and, in fact, weaker. In the cases of charism, charisma, and charismatic leadership, their original meanings contain insights and understandings that are far richer for an understanding of leadership than the accumulation of assigned but artificial meanings in recent leadership studies. Studies on charismatic leadership increased toward the end of the nineties and into the first decade of 2000. At times the studies seemed to offer little distinction between inspired and charismatic leadership.[1]

Charismatic leaders are people with special gifts that are used for the building up of the community. They acknowledge that these gifts come from God and imply call and responsibility. They also appreciate that other people are gifted and form part of a gifted or charismatic community. The prophetical leader emphasizes what the community ought to be; he or she proclaims what the vision of promise is. The mystical leader experiences how we ought to live as a community and even has an organizational expression of the values of hope and shares this experience with others. The charismatic leader has gifts that anticipate the best of the vision of promise and by living them in the present helps us move to the hope in which we believe. The prophet shares the word, the mystic experiences it, and the charismatic receives the gift.

1. "THE GREATER GIFTS" (1 COR 12:31)

For people who believe and hope, leadership is a gift, rooted in an understanding of community and organizational growth that is essentially the gift and work of God. Authority and leadership are delegated by the Author of the vision of hope. However, charisms and charismatic leadership are also delegated forms of authority. The term "charism" comes from St. Paul and basically means "gift of grace." The term occurs seventeen times in the New Testament, fourteen of them in Paul's writings, especially his letters to the Corinthians. A charism is "a spiritual gift," "bestowed on us by God"; its purposes include building up the community and enriching the common good. Everyone has some gift that can help the whole group. "But each has a particular gift from God, one having one kind and another a different kind." These gifts are manifestations of the power of God at work in the community for the attaining and implementing of the vision of hope.[2]

Paul's teachings on charisms have two focuses; first, everyone has a gift that serves to enrich others—in other words, Paul envisions a charismatically structured community; second, although there are a variety of gifts, some are greater and have a major impact on the direction of organizational life—in other words, Paul acknowledges that certain individuals are exceptional charismatic leaders. Paul juxtaposes four terms—spiritual gifts, gifts of grace, ministries, and activities—four aspects of a charismatically organized group (1 Cor 12:1–6). On another occasion, to stress his conviction that charisms are gifts of God, he parallels three forms of charisms with the actions of the God as their source. "Now there are varieties of gifts, but the same Spirit; and there are varieties of services, but the same Lord; and there are varieties of activities, but it is the same God who activates all of them in everyone" (1 Cor 12:4–6).

On four occasions, the letters list charisms that can enrich any organization;[3] the fact that the lists vary could indicate differences in local communities. All these charisms are signs of God's presence, actualizing the vision of hope and promise. They are gifts granted by God to assure healthy community life, and they encompass every aspect of community life. Some promote the growth of understanding, some the social, pastoral, and practical enrichment of life, others the physical health and well-being of the group, and still others the spiritual growth of the members. While Paul values every charism that enriches the life of the community, he ranks some to be more important than others, and he encourages his readers to "strive for the greater gifts" (1 Cor 12:31).[4]

Paul's understanding of charisms introduces a new spirit into organizational life. Every member of a community has gifts to share, every member recognizes others' gifts, and everyone appreciates that at times singular leaders arise who are especially gifted. These latter can be found at any level in an organization, but they have authority based on their gifts and not their position. They will need humility of the servant leader, as they use their gifts for the benefit of others, and do so with generosity, zeal, and cheerfulness. People are not passive in receiving these gifts. They have responsibility to prepare themselves, identify their own gifts, test them, use them well, and show responsibility to the community.[5] The presence of these gifts gives the community hope.

Paul is convinced that the variety and the mutual appreciation of each other's gifts enriches the community and is the basis for the involvement of everyone in organizational life. "We have gifts that differ according to the grace given to us: prophecy in proportion to faith; ministry, in ministering; the teacher, in teaching; the exhorter, in exhortation; the giver, in generosity; the leader, in diligence; the compassionate, in cheerfulness" (Rom 12:6–8). Every member of the community has a call, a commission, a gifted presence, an ability to influence others for good, and an opportunity to be a channel of grace to others. This is why Paul, following the above statement on the variety of gifts, describes the community as a human body made up of many parts. The body functions well when every part does its own job. Likewise in a gifted community, "There may be no dissension within the body, but the members may have the same care for one another. If one member suffers, all suffer together with it, if one member is honored, all rejoice together with it" (1 Cor 12:25–26).

Individuals who believe they have received spiritual gifts should evaluate carefully whether their gifts are from God for the hope-filled benefit of the group. As we will see, there are good charismatic leaders and there are bad ones. Paul insists we must discern the source and the use made of these gifts. First, we must ask ourselves serious questions: are we living in faith, are we open to the call of Christ within us, can we meet daily challenges with fidelity, do we persevere in the truth (2 Cor 13:5–8), does our vision of life include the spiritual and transcendent (1 Cor 2:14)?; then maybe our gifts are genuine. Then we should check around us in community. "Do not quench the Spirit. Do not despise the words of the prophets, but test everything: hold fast to what is good" (1 Thess 5:19–21). This need to discern the Spirit is also found in other New Testament writings. "Beloved, do not believe every spirit, but test the spirits to see whether they are from God; for many false prophets have gone out into the world" (1 John 4:1).[6] Genuine charisms complement each other, enrich the community, and unify the members (1 Cor 12:4–7). If all these check out well, then maybe the community gifts are genuine.

Charisms are God's gifts to a community to help it live in anticipation of the vision of promise; they are signs of the authenticity of hope. We must understand that the gift implies a calling (Rom 11:29), we must strive to understand and use our gifts (1 Cor 2:12), and we must know gifts are to be used with love (1 Cor 14:1). Although God is the giver of these leadership qualities, each one has an active role to play, for each one must be "eager for spiritual gifts" (1 Cor 14:12), "strive for the greater gifts" (1 Cor 12:31), and "excel in them" (1 Cor 14:12). With these comments Paul indicates that a person is not born with these gifts, so there is no "great person theory" here. Rather, one prepares, strives, is eager, and may be rewarded with gifts the community needs. The marvelous diversity of gifts enriches everyone in community. Thus, everyone assumes responsibility for the gifts received and shares them generously. The gifts must be for the common good and not disruptive of community well-being (1 Cor 14:26–33). Paul's views are clear; believers must appreciate they are part of a charismatic or gifted community and that at times specially gifted charismatic individuals lead the community. His views are true at any level of organizational life, and good leaders will always be sensitive to their own and to others' gifts, acknowledging the authority of gifts, and organize all for the shared benefit of all.

The original meaning of charism comes from a faith-filled community that believes it has received as gifts from God all the qualities necessary for its well-being and growth. Everyone has a gift that needs to be appreciated; some are specially gifted to lead. A charismatic leader could be at any level in the organization but has authority based on persuasion rather than on position. A key need is that everyone carefully tests the source and authenticity of gifts and that they mutually appreciate each other's gifts and thus create a new approach to organizational life. Leaders in particular must "strive for the greater gifts" (1 Cor 12:31).

2. ENTHUSIASM IN AN UNINSPIRED WORLD

Does anyone in this world want leadership as usual? Look at the leadership disasters we face on a daily basis in politics, business, health care, and religion! We have people in positions of great authority who do not have any leadership abilities. They gain their positions through money, careerism, patronage, ideological nepotism, or group need to preserve the status quo. They lack the most elementary gifts of leadership and do enormous damage to the organizations they are supposed to be serving. We have so many incompetent leaders that we become enthralled with a little leadership when we see it. We refer to people as charismatic or inspirational when they evidence the minimum signs of communication and organizational skills; when so many are incompetent and boring, a little inspirational speech seems remarkable!

Some people refer to individuals as charismatic when they inspire an audience, articulate vague ideas, find resonance and response in needy followers, and somehow focus on people's basic hopes. These often narcissistic individuals can be arrogant and generally vague, and play on followers' needs. It is little wonder that one author refers to charismatic authority as a "collective illusion."[7] In this view there is nothing special in the leader except in the opinion of followers. Such pseudocharismatics rarely offer details, show no ability to implement their goals, and offer no solutions to real problems. They can manipulate followers' views of them and use behaviors and skills that reinforce followers' views of their presumed competence and uniqueness.[8]

Frequently, a pseudocharismatic arrogantly imposes a worldview on followers. Their inspiration is an amputation of the Spirit, an empty illusion that moves uncritical people with media success. Of course, vague mission statements are useless even when enthusiastically presented. Good people are in this category as well as bad. The latter can cultivate the "collective illusion," provide dramatic, artificial rituals to enhance it, and repeat trigger concepts and catch phrases to focus attention on vague hopes. They give "important presentations" that treat of nothing significant. Some are harmless in the long term, but others present the demonic danger of arrogant leaders with charisma. Among the former are many contemporary leaders; among the latter are individuals like Hitler, Mao Tse Tung, Jim Jones, and David Koresh.

Humility, gratitude for the gifts received, and a dedication to surface the community's gifts characterize genuine charismatic leadership. It includes inspiration, motivation, enthusiasm, channeling of others' energy, focusing followers' attention, and a passion in the pursuit of shared goals. Charismatic leadership can be proactive or reactive, permanent or transitory; it can be for the life of the leader or for a simple episode in the community's development. What an institution recognizes as charismatic and who actually is charismatic will often differ. Some will be an integral part of a structure; others could be professional irritants who have the gift of stimulating followers into seeing what the right thing to do is. Both are of value to the community; one is integral to the institution and inspires it to move forward and the other is a free voice challenging the system to be different.

Authentic charismatic leadership has a social function, always implies responsibility and action, and realizes itself in community service. The charismatic must jealously guard his or her status as a free voice and resist authorities' fearful efforts to control and domesticate his or her challenge. However, the message of charismatic leadership must find resonance and acceptance from followers; otherwise the charismatic authority ceases to exist. Moreover, any leader who thinks he or she is charismatic but does not recognize a charismatic community is inauthentic.

The individual charismatic leader is generally considered to be a person of extraordinary qualities that are beyond those of ordinary followers and are appreciated as gifts of God for the benefit of the whole community. These leaders are often very intelligent, strong in spirit, with a more than ordinary ability to articulate their causes and persuade others. They can respond to crisis or to the felt needs of their followers, and they have a sense of the future.[9] Such an individual gains authority from the gifts he or she possesses. These gifts are used to articulate the values, mission, and goals of the community in light of the vision of God. When a charismatic leader speaks, followers should recognize their own hopes in the leader's vision. However, while challenging followers to question the community's direction, an authentic charismatic will always assure followers that they are free to question his or her vision as well.[10]

A leader of hope is essentially a mystic, always in union with God's vision for humanity. At times such a leader will be prophetical and at times also charismatic. Charismatic, mystical, and prophetical leaders can be different, but they mutually verify each other's message. While mystical leadership is a permanent feature of life, prophetical and charismatic leadership are episodic, even though often lasting a considerable time. When individuals think themselves to be prophets or charismatics, their leadership tends to become autocratic. Arrogant charismatics seek other people's conformity to their vision. Their passion is for their own way of viewing things, and they are distant from their followers, often maintaining that sense of separation through fear. Humble charismatics seek to spiritually energize others; their passion is for others' freedom and growth, and they are closely linked to their followers, constantly evidencing empathy and mutual support.

The prophet proclaims how things ought to be in the present; the charismatic focuses on how things can be in the future. Charismatic leadership is essentially motivation, establishing interest, using the gift of appealing and persuading, mobilizing others, generating shared hopes, animating followers, and enthusing and exciting them to pursue the vision of hope. Charismatic leaders generally have excellent communication skills, a compelling presence, and passion that draws others. Followers must recognize their trust, integrity, self-forgetfulness, appreciation of everyone's gifts, compassion, persevering fortitude, and a spirit of selfless service. Charismatic leaders can model what they call for, provide ideal images that attract and give hope, set high expectations of achievement, motivate for complex challenging tasks, show high levels of confidence in followers, and above all love them and develop their capacity to love while always respecting their freedom. They can do these things because of their vision of hope and because of their hope in their followers.

However, charismatic leadership is not enough by itself. It also requires practical implementation for authentic institutional transformation. These latter skills may also be part of the charismatic's gifts, but it can also be the case that someone else implements, and the charismatic, having inspired and motivated others, then leaves the scene. It is not enough to have vision and charismatic gifts; one must also find foresight, planning, and strategic skills.[11] Thus, a strength of the humble charismatic leader is that he or she appreciates being a part of a charismatic community and of discovering complementary gifts in others. A charismatic leader knows that critical knowledge for the future of the organization is not found in one person but spread throughout the charismatic community. Charismatic leadership is a response to a spiritual calling; one becomes a channel to others for "the descent of grace" and hope.[12] The humble leader will need to wait patiently and be available for the time when this spiritual gift comes from on high. Their hopes are beyond those of their followers; they are dreamers who can enlarge their own dreams with the dreams of others.[13]

It is increasingly common to find many men and women in leadership positions who are boring and incompetent. When a little leadership appears, we rush to declare the person inspiring and charismatic. Unfortunately, such people are often narcissistic and arrogant, and their followers are comfortably deceived. Genuine charismatics have extraordinary qualities but are humble; they serve the community, inspiring it to its future calling. Charisms can be long term, are frequently short term, and must be complemented by the usual skills of leadership.

3. CHARISMATIC LEADERS

1. Nurture Values of the Spirit

Charisms are gifts, but a leader can prepare himself or herself to be ready when the gift is offered. One does this by nurturing the values of the Spirit. St. Paul, in his letter to the Galatians, tells us, "The fruit of the Spirit is love, joy, peace, patience, kindness, generosity, faithfulness, gentleness, and self-control" (Gal 5:22). These are the qualities of charismatic leaders, and with these they build up the spirit of an organization. Moreover, if a leader is to be the source of other values such as inspiration, influence, optimism, enthusiasm, and excitement, then he or she must embody these values. Leaders can often do this because they trust people and the world around them; they have confidence and hope in God's direction of history; they have a sense of grace and of being loved for no reason in particular; they are always open to something new; they are people of integrity; they can balance the intuitive and rational realms of consciousness; and they long for the vision of the future.[14] These leaders live in the fear of the Lord, a fear that is learned from wisdom, not the result of a fright. Their hearts are open to the values of the Spirit, and their enthusiasm and spiritual energy generate a sense of mystery in their leadership.

One nurtures the values of the Spirit in reflection, inspirational reading, shared discussions with like-minded leaders, and prayer. This requires an openness of heart, an appreciation of beauty, a liberty of spirit, and a dedication to goodness. The charismatic leader not only leads well; he or she also lives well—a model of leadership's best values, a model of the best values of humanity. So the daily priorities of a charismatic leader are different from those of one who is not. He or she creates opportunities for contemplation, gives quality time to all members of his or her staff, reads material that uplifts the spirit, and patiently and kindly brings healing to any hurts in the organization.

2. Listen to the Gentle Reminders of the Spirit

Leaders today must be great listeners, not only to formal and informal input of others, but also to what motivates, inspires, and satisfies others. A leader must listen to others' felt needs, imagination, and dreams, especially when they refer to change or alternative ways of seeing things.[15] The charismatic leader receives his or her gifts from

73

God but often receives them through others as well, and so is always listening to what he or she can learn next. Such a leader is a peak performer, continually open to new ideas, new insights into vision, and new ways of actualizing the dream. In practice, this means giving full attention to others, showing genuine interest and concern in their ideas, dialoguing skillfully, delegating with sincerity, treating others' reports and plans with enthusiasm, evaluating with care, and critiquing with compassion.

A great listener listens to self, others, organizations, industry developments, and markets, but also to the signs of the times, the hopes of humanity, the yearnings of the needy, and the world's cries for help. Sometimes one can listen to and learn from the loud voices of our world. On other occasions one can listen to the gentle word of the Spirit in others' frustrations, in people's reactions to failed decisions and practices, in followers' rejoicing in organizational successes, in the hopes of the discriminated and oppressed, and in the stories and cries of those who suffer. A charismatic leader learns to listen to voices from wherever they come. A good leader also critically listens to his or her own ideas, own heart, own doubts, and own body.

3. Be Open and Receptive to What Life Brings

A gifted leader knows the best qualities of life are those he or she has received, and consequently appreciates the need to be open and receptive to what life brings. There is an ongoing youthfulness about a leader with charisms, an excitement regarding what could happen next, and a constant openness to hope. However, drive and determination give way to reflective time, a quieting of one's spirit, a restful aloneness that readies one to receive, and an awareness of one's emptiness and need. The charismatic leader can sit still, do nothing, relax, and intensify the uses of his or her senses: seeing, hearing, tasting—all ways of concentrating on what life brings. Looking so intensely, he or she sees things never seen before; listening so carefully, he or she hears sounds never noticed before; tasting so thoroughly, he or she savors flavors never experienced before. This is a training to concentrate and appreciate many aspects of daily life.

Some contemporary leaders in all forms of organizational life are so full of themselves, so confident of the little they know, so certain of their grasp of the vision, so messianic in the roles they assume, that they are incapable of learning and are destined to be ignorant and incompetent for life. Charismatic leaders are open and receptive to God, others, the environment, social trends, and the cries of humanity. They are great because of the gifts they have received; they will be continually great because of what they will receive in the future.

4. Be Grateful for the Gifts of Life

Leaders should have a positive mental attitude and a healthy self-esteem. They know their gifts, appreciate them, and can thus expect more of themselves. Gratitude is a special quality of a charismatic leader. He or she is enthused about the community's many gifts and becomes a focal point of expressions of gratitude to all. Colleagues and followers know the leader appreciates them, and they give more of themselves, knowing the leader will receive their dedication with gratitude. In fact, the leader of hope can be grateful for dedicated work, even though it leads to failure.

The leader will create opportunities to celebrate the successes of others, either informally while passing someone in the corridor, or more formally in community celebrations. They do this with a naturalness that proclaims genuine gratitude. "Employee of the month" does not cut it anymore. Rather, the leader will keep well informed about employees' achievements, thus always having reasons to say something positive, affirming, and grateful. Likewise, the leader will be a link between those above and those below in the organization, creating a mutually appreciative approach to all. They will also be grateful for customers, subcontractors, shareholders, and trustees. These attitudes do not exclude the critical assessments that need to be made, nor do they exclude the normal successful leadership and management skills that the charismatic leader will always need. However, gratitude is basic and fundamental to all that the leader does.

5. *Discern the Presence of Goodness*

The leader must choose freely from alternatives, selecting what is the best and leaving aside what is not. This will include flexibility, creativity, imagination, and innovation to reframe issues to discover the best. While organizations often dislike change, the leader must encourage followers to question, challenge, analyze alternatives, and be courageous enough to change.[16] The charismatic leader trains followers for healthy skepticism, constructive criticism, and forceful hope. In times of uncertainty, some reactions will be merely transitional correctives, but they will help move the organization to discern its true direction. There is goodness in every aspect of life. Negative developments can have good side effects; obstacles we encounter have potentialities for good. In a world that stresses negativity, a charismatic leader who has experienced the goodness of God's gifts focuses on goodness wherever it can be found. This not only transforms his or her approach to life but also the approach to leading others in organizational life.

Discernment is not haphazard or episodic. It is a definite methodology for group assessment that leaders use for making major decisions that affect the organization's future. It includes serious, reflective evaluation of each alternative response to the issues in discussion. It is done with respect for the opinions of each person who presents input on which others reflect rather than giving immediate counterpositions. Members evaluate the pros and cons of each position before presenting their mature evaluation. Gradually the leader moves the group toward consensus.

6. Be Humble in All You Do

The charismatic leader is a leader of hope. "Hope charts a course between despair and presumption, recognizing that if we are not yet there we are on the way. The virtue of ongoing youthfulness, hope makes us confident without being arrogant and humble without self-contempt."[17] Such a leader will need determination, perseverance in efforts, and courage to plow ahead to new goals. The sense of confidence will need to be balanced with humility, for people have given up on arrogant, overbearing leaders. Today's leader lives with uncertainty, knows he or she no longer has the answers, is ready to accept new ways of doing things, and appreciates that the best ideas can come from anywhere in the organization. Aware that everyone has gifts of one kind or another, he or she gives people confidence to act with authority.

Charismatic leaders need to be particularly careful to be humble about their own views. When many become arrogant and domineering about their own ideas, clinging to their own ways of doing things and manipulative of others, the genuine charismatic must scrutinize his or her own ideas, focus on other people's contributions, and always give credit to others whenever possible. The leader should push authority away from self to others, stop making all the decisions, and get out of other people's way as they work for the common good.

7. Cherish Others and Their Gifts

Organizational goals are best achieved by communities in which each member feels valued. Success depends on knowledge, motivation, team spirit, coordination of activities, and a common community spirit. The leader of hope knows that vision may well come from followers and be merely articulated by the charismatic individual who discerned the gifts of followers and acted on them. The leader has to really care about other people, help them continually through example, and have a passion for their success. "In general, these leaders believe that people perform best when they feel good about themselves and their work, they try to create situations that contribute to that feeling."[18] When followers know they are trusted and admired, they are motivated to do more in giving their discretionary commitment and thus exceed what was expected of them. This collegial approach is part of being a charismatic community.

As part of valuing other people and their contributions, a leader will strive for inner integrity to be the genuine person his or her followers deserve. The leader will model the values for which others should strive, set an example that others can emulate, and treat everyone with respect, dignity, and justice. The leader who cherishes others will create a climate of mutual trust, coach and guide them, influence them to be visionaries, foster their self-leadership, and inspire the commitment to the community's shared vision.[19]

8. Be a Gift to Others

A good leader influences others to exceed themselves. He or she gives followers a sense of their own maturity and wisdom in leadership. Charisms can be shared even at different levels. The leader can give others the opportunities to utilize their gifts. Delegation, collaboration, shared mission values, subsidiarity, and empowering individuals and teams are all ways to give others the space and occasions to grow and appreciate their own gifts.

Being a gift to others also means being a good leader. Hope is an attitude to leadership, but the skills must be there as well. The leader must prepare self to be well qualified, to maintain the quality of the goods or services the organization offers, to establish just procedures for hiring, evaluation, and due process, and to implement the organization's code of ethics.

More than anything else, the charismatic leader is a gift to others in showing love and encouragement. Always more effective than adversarial roles, love builds up others and gives meaning to their lives. "Love means service, mentoring, seeing the world from others' points of view, making others successful. It means compassion. Love also means validation."[20] A charismatic leader is who he or she is because of a gift of love—the charism received. Their whole life is to be modeled on self-gift in loving service to others. They appreciate that selfless love of others makes sense. The vocation of hope-filled leadership is "faith working through love" (Gal 5:6); this is the charismatic leader's daily choice.

CHAPTER SIX

LEADERSHIP AND HEALING

I
S it possible to lead people, communities, or organizations without having a healing effect on them? No, obviously not! The prophetical leader focuses on the authenticity and integrity of the vision and message; the mystical leader on an understanding of organizational life that emerges from a profound experience of humanity's calling; the charismatic leader on the many, mutually authenticating gifts of the community; and the healing leader on the universal need of redemption. There is, in fact, an intimate link between leadership and healing.

1. STRIVING FOR WELLNESS

We often speak about service and leadership and even servant leadership, but the original word " to serve" in Greek, the language of the New Testament, was the word "therapy," which expressed the idea of leading, serving, taking care of, and healing. Jesus' leadership had two components or facets: teaching and healing. If teaching was the content of his vision, it was authenticated in healings. But "to heal" (*sozo* in Greek) means to protect from harm, to benefit, to preserve inner integrity, to rescue from harm; these are all aspects of Jesus' leadership that save and redeem. Leading and healing are two aspects of the same reality that focuses on integrated, holistic approaches to people and their organizations. Leadership that heals restores harmony within individuals, between people, and within structures. Leadership that heals frees from the bonds of sickness and the demons of unhealthy living.

Health and wholeness are basic, primary values for all human beings, and people see sickness and dysfunctional responses as undesirable obstacles to happiness and fulfillment in life. When health and wholeness are absent, people seek explanations and remedies, and when these are not forthcoming, they suspect that there are forces beyond themselves working against them. Whatever the explanation of sickness, people long for healing. A leader of hope who is attentive to organizational dysfunctioning should feel called to heal. He or she must be sensitive to others' needs, be a voice for the voiceless, and stress that successful organizations require holistic living. A leader of hope who wants to have a healing effect on an organization must listen to workers' stories and anger, call them to community health and wellness, and teach how wellness, leisure, health, personal or organizational growth, and business effectiveness are closely related to each other.

In dealing with others and organizations, leaders strive for wellness, a concept that means the best one can be at any given time. Individuals and organizations come with the baggage of their history, and a good leader cannot expect from followers immediate exemplary responses to his or her challenges. The first stage in healing is to stop negative influences, the slow erosion of values, and the corrupt influences of power. Healing also includes efforts to end destructive practices such as confrontational positions; neglect of workers; coercion of followers; harassment; paying for support; outright fraud; controlling management teams with salaries or threats regarding job security; dividing to conquer; and using people rather than collaborating with them. A leader who heals confronts any crisis of quality, changes in standards, and neglect of traditional values, and does so because he or she recognizes that we are all capable of evil, we often know our flaws and do nothing about them, we live with false values or reduced ideals, and we need illumination and healing.

Wellness is more than the absence of dysfunctions in individuals and organizations. It is a holistic concept that includes physical, social, and spiritual components. People can work at wellness through self-motivation and healthy practices. Components of wellness include a positive outlook on life, basic personal and organizational skills, a sense of purpose, respect and love for each other, being in tune with one's environment, and having a plan for balanced living. Like other aspects of organizational life, a leader can manage wellness.

A leader who heals gives special attention to emotions, whether job- or people-related, identifying causes and potential reactions, and making sure he or she channels positive emotions and controls negative ones. Among the former are acceptance, joy, trust, surprise, and satisfaction; and among the latter are fear, anger, hatred, rage, pride, jealousy, sadness, and loss.[1] Each of these has many manifestations. For example, people can have fear of failure, of embarrassment, of disappointing others, of resentment of leaders, of lack of respect, and of losing self-confidence.[2] Leadership is almost impossible for those who lack the ability to react to these emotions. Leaders of hope partner with followers, understand their emotions, and raise them up to their potential. They have faith in their followers, see that they attain their own hopes and contribute to the organization's, and love them enough to seek what is best for them.[3]

Anything that negatively affects the well-being of individuals or organizations needs healing. At times people's negative reactions and attitudes belie explanations other than the mystery of life and the problem of evil. First, leaders will be shocked at some negativity; second, they will become conscious of the damage sick attitudes can do to others and to the organization; and third, they will dedicate themselves to action that reforms, liberates, redeems, and transforms. Wellness requires healing at three levels: physical—changing the environment and stopping harassment and all forms of oppression; psychological—working for human dignity in its many personal and social aspects; and moral-spiritual—channeling purpose and human fulfillment.

Jesus taught the Golden Rule: treat others as you would like them to treat you. This leads to mutual healing. Buddha offered the eight-fold noble path to eliminate all suffering and bring healing. This focused on right attitudes to self, others, and one's vision in life. Leaders throughout history—religious and others—insist that the healing process is essentially a transformation of mind and heart. It implies acknowledging evil, undoing harm, making whole, and opening self and others to the challenges of a future of hope. While old approaches to leadership implied power, control, and dominance, leaders of hope are forgiving, reconciling, healing, loving, and enabling. For a great leader of hope, healing self, others, and organizations is a journey to the values deep within one's heart; it is essentially a redirection of life to compassionate care.

A leader of hope constantly asks what individuals and the organization would be like if all were functioning well. The organization's product or service, its workers, management, and structure should all perform well. This does not mean that there are not irritants in the group who do not think or act the way others do. They, too, receive healing acceptance and affirmation, for the group needs energy that comes from differences. Wellness within an organization will include trust, ethics, protection within the working environment, truth telling, financial integrity, mutual respect, mutual pride, patience with each other, and a sense of responsibility for each other and for the organization.

2. LEADERS AS HEALERS

1. Leaders Heal Themselves

The primary focus of healing leadership is the self-healing of the leader who, like everyone else, yearns for wholeness. History shows us leaders who have led followers to atrocities, violence, hatred, division, and polarization. But even locally many leaders diminish and become less than they could be because of their own leadership styles.

Some leaders are immersed in denial, arrogance, and deceit, and their leadership makes them inhuman. Domineering, arrogant, greedy leaders create victims everywhere. In many organizations, the boss who is responsible for vision, values, and standards has no sense of responsibility, no vision, no values, and no standards. Much contemporary organizational disease that cries out for healing results from inauthentic, that is, sick ways of thinking and desiring.[4] Other leaders at least become aware of a gnawing sense of regret for their leadership failures. Leaders must heal themselves of their own failures and bring harmony into their own lives.

So much pseudoleadership today is a festering wound that must be cleansed and disinfected before it will ever heal. An individual leader must always appreciate that he or she needs healing in order to effectively serve others and the organization. Perhaps leaders should take an oath similar to that of physicians: first do no harm. Some so-called leaders can only have a healing influence on the organization by resigning. There are situations that cannot be healed, such as those that arise from deliberate evil and unethical decisions of a controlling boss. These individuals may need psychological counseling before change is possible. Healing self from greed, ambition, and controlling attitudes needs self-discipline, temperance, a focus on others, a new view of self, and a new commitment to integrity.

A leader who wishes to heal others needs self-care, a healthy lifestyle, and behavioral changes where appropriate. He or she also needs to appreciate the meaning of life, have some personal understanding of suffering and sickness, appreciate the benefits of personal healing, and be open to the healing effects of others. Once a person understands his or her own need of healing, he or she can then appreciate the advantages of healing for others. A leader then hopes for personal change and for others' change too.

A leader of hope must also deal with the negativity and pain that come with leading others. At times, leaders work with awkward and difficult employees, suffer the stress and even agony of decision making, and face the anguish of attempting to resolve gut-wrenching situations. They must cope with the personally felt consequences of job stress, burnout, accidents, harassment, terminations, losses to the organization when workers retire, and even the pressures of success. Leaders frequently need to deal with their own pain and with the pain of others, and find that leadership can impact one's health, relationships, sense of purpose, and fulfillment. They can be dedicated to community and feel lonely. Of course, a sick organization makes good leaders of hope sick too, unless they can steel themselves against it.

Healing self in these situations is part of the ongoing conversion of a leader. It means overcoming personal sin, even the small tendencies to selfishness that tend to weaken one's wholehearted commitment. A leader's journey is away from self-centeredness to self-transcendence and to a focusing on the importance of others. It includes removing prejudice and being open to others, listening more and talking less, being more attentive and less distracted, valuing others more and judging them less, and centering on the legacy of others and not on one's own. It will also include working for trust and never presuming it, telling the truth and living the truth in love, communicating well and clarifying positions and values, guaranteeing others their own space, and maintaining a vision of high hopes amid the mini-despairs. The training of leaders to self-healing includes integrity, honesty, breaking down barriers, releasing others' potential, and being magnanimous in dealing with others.[5] Healing of self is a redirection of one's mind and heart.[6]

2. Leaders Have a Healing Influence on Others

A hope-filled leader knows healing is needed when individuals focus exclusively on self-interest, exhibit excessive internal competition, constantly engage in comparisons with others, evidence mutual blame, lose vitality, compromise their integrity, and deliberately do things they know are unethical. A leader also recognizes the need for healing when some in the organization are always marginalized, when there are voiceless members, and when there is widespread indifference to others' needs. Healing is clearly needed when administration restricts communication, misuses power, allows significant disparity in executives' salaries, and governs autocratically. When managers enter and leave the organization with increased salaries and golden parachutes, having done nothing significant, then the organization and its board members need healing. When managers simply do not try to slow the erosion of values, then they also need healing.

Every organization has some individuals in pain, feeling loss, experiencing broken relationships at work and at home, and suffering from a lack of meaning; and this sense of pain affects the quality of their work. In fact, some within an organization need healing but do not know it. Then again some sick individuals make everyone else sick without ever feeling anything themselves. A leader of hope has to heal the wounds caused by former bosses and also by coworkers. Some individuals adapt themselves to sick situations and then become as sick as everyone else. No organization can function well amid unhealthy situations that sap vitality, creativity, and commitment. This is one of the challenges of a leader of hope.

A leader of hope allows no one to feel inferior but raises people up to their just level of appreciation. Healing others is a major task of a leader of hope who thus enables others to become their complete selves. This includes healing relationships within organizations, clarifying and refocusing roles, setting goals together, making sure channels of communication are open, reflecting on each other's gifts, and expressing recognition and appreciation of everyone's contribution.

The leader's healing influence will vary for each member in need. Some may feel they are taken for granted, and a leader must give them visibility and prominence. For others who have been the object of bogus empowerment by previous leaders, a leader of hope must give genuine, significant delegation. There are always members who feel used, often because they are, and a leader will need to heal by letting people feel at home in the organization and making them objects of sincere admiration and respect.

A good leader creates for those within an organization a healthy way of living together, and this implies risk taking. He or she will encourage others to get involved in the journey to wholeness, to share in common values, to become vulnerable as he or she manifests genuine emotions of heart and love. Part of a healthy way of living together is to heal the loneliness of all around us, to awaken others to hope, to enable people to resolve conflicts constructively, and to move them by making it clear that they are loved.

Leaders of hope restore others to healing through listening, empathy, compassion, even a sense of humor, healing broken relationships, restoring justice, and building a reconciling community. A leader of hope will focus on values of colleagues, since a person without values causes problems for others. Then the insidious destruction of the vision of hope causes everyone·to live a reduced notion of what it means to be human.

3. Leaders of Hope Heal Organizations

Leaders constantly ask themselves what the true nature of the organization is and what its purpose in the vision of God is, and when it is not normal they know it needs healing. Some organizations are immersed in global hopelessness; some multinationals respond to no one. These need to be exorcized of their false values and their diminished notions of dignity, love, justice, community, and human fulfillment. Some need healing in matters of ethics. Often we put bandages on the failures of organizational life, but that is insufficient; we must heal them and enable them to become their best. However, for every leader it is difficult but necessary to heal and lead to wholeness his or her own small organization, when all around is organizational sickness, disintegration, and decay of values.[7]

Healing begins with the mind and heart, values, vision, mission, and structures. If a leader inherited a sick organization, he or she will need to put together the brokenness, remove unjust structures, and challenge an unhealthy, oppressive working environment. A leader will need to identify the casualties of sick organizations and sick decisions. Much sickness in organizational life is disharmony, a loss of balance. Every organization must face up to its own problems and the pathological aspects of its false values. Some organizations have a cult of personality for its managers that a good leader will correct and purify. Others have false drive, artificial intensity, and oppressive stressful situations.

A leader of hope heals the structural components of the change process, moving them away from prideful centralization and its careerism to focus on healing teams, establishing collegial structures, and instituting collaborative planning. Mediocrity must always be the object of healing. Redeveloping and improving product or service quality, balancing the budget, increasing profit—all can entail false priorities that cry out for healing.

The psychological reasons for a group's formation and development—the justification for an individual's membership—include the need of liberation, the desire of social adaptation, and the probability of success. When these are left thwarted, individuals become dissatisfied, frustrated, and unfulfilled. A leader of hope focuses on the deficiencies and channels people's rediscovered hopes. In doing so, he or she heals memories of organizational betrayal and redeems an institution that otherwise might die. When a leader heals an organization, people's needs are met again, and as they mature they contribute to meeting others' needs and renewing the organization.

3. PRESCRIPTIONS FOR HEALING LEADERSHIP

1. Name the Dysfunction That Needs Healing

Dysfunction arises in individuals for a variety of reasons. Some people because of psychological or character flaws deliberately do what they know is wrong. Others are ignorant of the human values that ought to be present in a vision of hope and promise, and they simply do not care. Still others are overwhelmed by collective social dysfunctions that generations accept as the normal order of the day, and while not intending wrong they are unconsciously a part of the human conditions. The first component of healing is a diagnostic phase, a process of discernment that identifies and names what needs to change. It is not difficult to name greed, selfishness, abuse of people or the economy, destruction of the common good, financial mismanagement, irresponsibility, a lack of professionalism, and so on. However, sometimes contemporary dysfunctional activities are difficult to identify. What is ethical or unethical is not as easy to identify as it used to be. We are often not dealing with incompetence but with the competence of evil and immoral attitudes. We must recognize and name the failures of the past and present, so that there emerges the chance of a better future.

2. Embrace Healing as a Function of Leadership

If the diagnosis is correct and a response is forthcoming, a leader can look forward to better workers, products, services, community, and human fulfillment. All within an organization can savor the opportunities for healing of attitudes and structures as part of a vision of hope. When healing is valued, the leader who serves others may want a personal healer to keep him or her on the track to healthy growth. Embracing healing includes the recognition that the organizational system is flawed, and it requires humility and a spirit of

89

repentance that implies a willingness to change. It includes welcoming the authentic meaning of the vision of hope that heals and renews. Embracing healing through personal and communal enlightenment is a form of ongoing renewal that can transform individuals and organizations. In a healing organization, work quality improves, absenteeism decreases, mutual appreciation increases, and common values are strengthened.

3. Take the Appropriate Remedies

Once a leader identifies problems, then he or she must utilize a variety of healing skills to remedy the dysfunction. Sometimes the leader will need therapeutic and leadership skills, often psychological and educational skills, and on occasion spiritual and community skills. All these can contribute to holistic health and wellness. Often a leader can use healing remedies only as needed, for the crisis will pass. At other times, the medication will be something taken every day to manage a more critical problem. In some organizations there are individuals who do extensive harm but will not contribute to their own healing. Keeping them in the organization only reduces the organization's overall health, and the leader will need to challenge such people firmly and compassionately, and as a last resort redirect such individuals elsewhere. The leader cannot neglect the common good, the greater good, and organizational harmony.

4. Do Things Because They Are Right

In recent decades we have witnessed so much wrongdoing by rogue individuals or groups and by organizations that we all long for a renewed commitment with high accountability.[8] We need an ethical revolution that will retrain leaders to do things because they are right and not just because they are profitable. Leaders need not ask can we do this or that, but should we. Ethics needs courage, and it needs leaders with spine. However, it is clear that good ethics pays; it is good business. And bad ethics can have a disastrous impact on the bottom line and on an organization's survival. We need leaders who will let good overtake evil. Clearly, this will require a healing of mindsets that have prevailed for too long with their destructive influences on so many.

5. Remove Artificiality and Work for Sincerity and Integrity

It would be difficult to affirm that the first decade of this millennium is a success from the point of view of leadership. There have been wonderful studies, research, and insights, but practice has lagged behind. We seem to have learned a lot about what leadership is not, rather than to have witnessed what it can and ought to be. Nowadays, many leaders have their spin doctors to cover up the realities of their failed leadership. We know political, business, and religious leaders more for their failures than their successes. However, it is useful to know what leadership is not, and we have been overwhelmed by insincerity, untruthfulness, constant cover-ups, extensive damage to people and organizations, and a total lack of integrity. Leadership needs a healing reform that can produce leaders of hope rather than managers of despair. Leaders must clean house and bring back values that assure the organization of long-term success. They must heal the organization of insincerity and of a lack of integrity.

6. Update the Organization's Values

Healing is often proactive. Values become old and no longer as effective as they were. They can contribute negatively to future development. Often an organization loses sight of its own mission, and leaders must help the organization recover its values. On other occasions, when values cease to be relevant, new values can start the process of organizational vision and mission once again. If common commitment to an organization's values is to have an ongoing healing influence, then it begins at the grassroots level of workers and their aspirations made real in values they cherish. These values form the basis of an enduring purpose that gives rise to a mission that leaders and followers can then embody in goals and strategies. Leaders cannot impose values but must discover them in people who then own them and will commit themselves to pursue them. "If you're going to stir the souls of your constituents, if you are going to lift them to a higher level of performance, then this is what you need to know: it's not the leader's vision, it's the people's vision that matters most."[9] While some leaders love their business techniques and unfortunately use people, leaders of hope love their people and their values and use techniques to make those values relevant.

7. Establish a Vision of Redemptive Justice

Leaders of hope bring about a future vision that overwhelms the sins of the past. So many leaders and organizations have been and are unjust to their workers, to their customers, to their shareholders. Likewise, workers can initiate demands that are unjust to others, and so can shareholders. Freedom within an organization is not a license to get away with whatever you can. Working for mutual justice has a redemptive effect on all who are involved. It is a multidimensional process that removes biases, bigotry, selfishness, and injustice, and constructs mutuality in respect, rights, hopes, and fulfillment. Leaders of hope accept the fact that it is unacceptable to make a profit based on injustice. Leaders of hope who dedicate themselves to healing strive to make decisions that are always just.

8. Create a Self-Healing Organization

It is not enough that a leader brings healing. Rather, he or she must develop self-healing among individuals and also for organizations. This will include the fostering of honest work, conscience formation, values of character, morality, genuine humanity, a spirit of sacrifice, and dedication to principles and integrity.[10] Hiring and evaluation procedures should incorporate administration competence but also skills in administering and leading in a healthy manner. This means creating an environment where healing is important—not just a safe environment for workers, a pleasant environment, but also an environment conducive to growth. Leaders who create self-healing organizations never belittle others, never criticize them publicly, never fail to give undivided attention, never become self-preoccupied, never play favorites, and never embarrass weak workers.[11] Many problems frequently found in organizations are diminished or absent in self-healing organizations where individuals feel at home, respected, and appreciated.

9. Bring about Personal and Organizational Conversion

Thinking of others and their well-being instead of oneself is the result of a movement from self-centeredness to self-transcendence. It is an aspect of conversion. This latter word means "a change of heart" and implies that the focus of one's heart and mind has changed, and one has surrendered self to a vision of hope. Organizations, too, can go through this moral and value movement that provokes new ways of thinking about their purpose in the life of the human community. Not everyone will respond with this personal and organizational conversion. Some will participate in the process; others will leave, unable to share this vision, and still others will remain but become a polarizing influence. Over a period of time the organization's vision self-selects followers and gradually consolidates its shared values. Conversion and healing are both ongoing realities in a vision of hope; they wax or wane together. The change we need today "is so dramatic that organizations must experience 'metanoia' [the word is Greek for "conversion"] or fundamental change. If organizations fail to become metanoic organizations, they cease to compete."[12]

10. Let Organizations Die When It Is Appropriate

In recent years we have seen how some organizations become immersed in wrongdoing, and individuals who know about it often do nothing. Rather, when there are evil situations, people should help the organization when possible, endeavoring to facilitate a transformational conversion. At times, however, the wrongdoing overwhelms the institution and it begins to fall apart. The problem generally lies with poor to nonexistent leadership. Unfortunately, people are often given authority and power way beyond their competence. We have seen presidents, CEOs, bishops, and other religious leaders who are simply not competent for the level of power they have, and there needs to be new structures in government, business, and religion to protect people from the arrogant and incompetent misuse of power. Of course, it also goes without saying that there generally are other structures that could bring balance, but they are not used. We need to get used to letting some institutions die when it is appropriate to do so. Keeping some on life-support is a disservice to everyone involved and maintains unhealthy organizations that daily harm good people.

CHAPTER SEVEN

PRACTICES TRANSFORMED BY HOPE

HOPE is a fundamental attitude that influences a leader's way of living and leading. He or she will continue to follow certain styles of leadership with behaviors, skills, and attitudes. Hope, however, modifies everything a leader does. A leader of hope links together the vision and skills of leadership with the vision and habits of hope. In this chapter we look at several good practices of a leader of hope, those things that leaders of hope do, those things that transform their leadership.

1. MOURN LEADERSHIP'S FAILURES

It is frequently heartbreaking to follow the daily news. We often find ourselves wanting to turn off the television, put down the paper, and switch off the computer so we do not have to follow it anymore. We know so much is wrong with our world, and most of it results from bad leadership. We see countries run by vicious, oppressive dictators; violence against women and children; genocide perpetrated and defended; torture accepted as policy; overwhelming oppression of the poor; national disasters mismanaged; wars of aggression that are unjust and immoral; failures of businesses with criminals at all levels; hypocrisy, inactivity, and blasphemy of religious leaders; judicial systems that still favor the wealthy and the connected; and national leaders who do nothing for their people. So many problems have lasted for decades; they are well known but deliberately left unaddressed.

We live in a culture of greed, addiction to power, and arrogance. We are immersed in malfunctioning and sick leadership, and the sickness is contagious. So much leadership breathes artificiality and falsehood. How many good people, even family and friends, have you seen sucked into the systemic corruption of contemporary leadership? Good people who live as well as they can, still work in organizations that cheat a little, waste a little, corrupt a little, and even oppress a little. Successes in leadership are so few; we must sadly conclude that failed leadership is the normal order of the day. Things could be so different if only we had good leadership. However, one cannot build new leadership on the foundations of recent years.

As leaders we must mourn our world of failed leadership. When we think about mourning, we refer to something that it pains us to think about; it is a loss that tears at our hearts; it is a pain that stays with us. You just wish things were different and what happened never occurred. So it is to mourn leadership's failures. Our mourning is not just intellectual, but emotional and spiritual; it is a loss beyond words, and we must first savor the pain before we can move on.

"Blessed are they who mourn, for they will be comforted" (Matt 5:4). As leaders we can be comforted, but the injustices and failures will remain until leadership itself changes. The basic steps in mourning leadership's failures are:

1. Acknowledge the failures.
2. Think about and even savor the harm bad leadership has done.
3. Disassociate yourself from it.
4. Examine your own life for traces of failures and get rid of them.
5. Express the sorrow of your heart for the harm and injustice done to others.

6. Move on with changed attitudes or move away from the corrupt structure in which you have found yourself.

"Leadership can be threatened by a dearth of positive models."[1] As leaders, each of us must daily live with the memories of harmful leadership. We should try to understand the motivation of failed leadership and the false values failed leaders promote. Understanding better, we must never take the first steps toward accepting the kinds of values and approaches to life that lead to such failed leadership.

Five Suggestions

1. As leaders, never support greedy, selfish, unethical leaders.
2. Beware of the company you keep, and stay away from people whose values you despise and whose leadership you do not wish to imitate.
3. Never accept promotion in your leadership if you must compromise your values to get it.
4. Every day spend some time thinking about those who suffer because of failed leadership.
5. Remind yourself often of your own failures as a leader and lament and mourn them.

2. APPRECIATE WHAT LIES BEYOND NORMAL HORIZONS

Some leaders are entrapped in the parameters they have established. They pace around inside their own cage, the stronger eating the weaker, and they call this success. Not only is there a world outside the narrow confines of current leaders, but genuine leadership is only found outside such confines. Other so-called leaders plod ahead like the Budweiser horses with blinders on, lest they be distracted by realities around them. The vision pursued by the leader of hope lies beyond normal horizons in the plan of God. Such a leader must have a facility in rising from daily occurrences to make connections to transcendent values. This is one of the most practical things anyone can do, for thinking of the vision of promise gives clear understanding and directives for daily life and leadership.

When you see someone being treated unjustly, ask yourself why you made such a conclusion. Are the links between right and wrong, justice and injustice, something you have a natural feel for? Why? Where did you get such judgment? What is the measure you are using? When you witness exploitation, abuse, oppression, profiting from underprivileged, making money from undocumented immigrants, why do you consider this abnormal? What should be normal? Why do you think you should treat others as you would wish to be treated? When you hear of bosses rotating from one job to another, barely coping with their responsibilities, but receiving obscene salaries until you can get rid of them so they will do no more damage, how do you think they ought to act and why do you think this? What is the purpose of all our efforts? We work, earn, live, retire; is this all there is? When you look at the emptiness and smallness of the world of organizational development, why are you appalled by some actions and impressed by others?

Some values seem to draw out the best in people. When you see you are loved by someone for no particular reason, you find that you are loveable and wonder why. Other people are loveable, too, for no particular reason except the fact that they exist. Why do we appreciate love so much and find it is right for everyone—not merited, but just right? Likewise, when you look beyond normal horizons of daily life, you appreciate justice, equality, love, interdependence, and goodness. Why?

Seeing what lies beyond normal horizons leads us to see and experience a loving God, and that experience changes all understandings of leadership. A leader of hope becomes ever more aware of the importance of love. "And now faith, hope, and love abide, these three; and the greatest of these is love" (1 Cor 13:13). The seeker encounters values beyond normal horizons, and this new focus produces inspirational leadership. The new approach to leadership is more expansive and is based on a worldview that includes transcendent values. "To successfully engage in leadership in the future, individuals and organizations will need to expand and revise their understanding of leadership and how they practice it."[2]

Some spiritual leaders and visionary mystics who have appreciated what lies beyond normal horizons of life speak of their vision as one of beauty. They refer to this self-immersion in values of love, justice, goodness, and so on, as an experience of beauty. John of the Cross, a dynamic individual to whom I have previously referred, speaks of seeking the beauty of God, experiencing a certain spiritual feeling of God's presence, and glimpsing God's way of dealing with humanity as something of beauty.[3] This beauty is not something visual but rather a glimpse into the harmony that exists in the vision of promise, a grasp of just how right everything is in the vision beyond the normal horizons of life—this is the vision for which the leader of hope strives every day.[4]

Five Suggestions

1. When faced with decisions, not only ask how, but also why.
2. Spend a little time each day in quiet reflection, empty of concerns and ready to receive.
3. Look at things that surprise you in life and ask why.
4. Think about why you are loved and loveable.
5. Ask yourself for answers to puzzling attitudes you meet in leaders you know.

3. THINK, MEDITATE, CONTEMPLATE

Leaders of hope are men and women of wisdom who make their judgments based on a combination of conceptual thinking, imaginative skills, an artistic sense, intuition, contemplative insight, and the system and community skills of love.[5] These components of decision making imply new ways of thinking, meditating, and contemplating. These leaders process information for judgment in more integrative ways and always in light of the vision of promise. Making practical judgments requires all the usual research and analysis, but it also becomes a work of art, of hope-filled critical analysis, and of love, thus integrating and reconciling efficiency with the vision of hope. "We must look at life through a kaleidoscope—to imagine possibilities outside of conventional categories, to envision actions that cross traditional boundaries, to anticipate repercussions and take advantage of interdependencies, and to make new connections or invent new combinations."[6]

Nowadays we no longer value leaders who can make snap judgments, but those who think things through and make correct judgments. We have no use for the so-called leader who makes those "tough" decisions, but one who thinks of every alternative and of everyone involved, and comes up with a decision that is hope-filled in difficult times. We value leaders who have intellectual curiosity.

The leader of hope is not satisfied only with thinking, but learns to discover and appreciate deeper levels of meaning through meditation. This latter is a discursive form of reflection; in quiet and peaceful recollection a person leaves aside prejudices and prior thought patterns and opens mind and heart to the pros and cons of each issue. This detached reflection process enables a leader to see the positive and negative aspects of decisions. No one has speedy answers to today's complicated issues in leadership; often it is not clear what is ethical and what is not, what is for long-term benefit and what is not, what is selfish and what is altruistic. One needs to ready one's heart and soul to make good decisions today.

Meditation is primarily an individual practice, but leaders can also achieve its basic purpose in group or team reflection on issues under discussion. As one practices meditation, it becomes less a method and more a simple way of calmly thinking things through. Moreover, the more one uses meditation with skill, the less it becomes an exercise of thought, and more one of love. "Overall, the process is one of calming the body and mind until intuitive wisdom comes through. Experience shows that the calmer we are, the more we have access to our creative and intuitive aspects. As we become calmer, we start to see dimensions of a problem we have never seen before."[7]

Meditation is discursive thought but gradually becomes a form of prayerful reflection on concrete matters to determine how things ought to be done according to the vision of promise. Gradually this process becomes simpler until it is a form of centering mind and heart on the issues. "A transformational leader perceives in a more inclusive way. Their vision extends to the inner depth of things. The light coming from the leader shines upon the object of inquiry and reveals its hidden pattern of being and becoming."[8] Once learned and practiced well, it takes less time and is similar to "centering prayer." Less and less discursive, one's heart detached from prejudices, one's whole being desirous of doing good, the leader of hope become contemplative in his or her approach to life's issues. Contemplation is nondiscursive; a more intuitive experience in which a prayerful leader just sees what is the right thing to do. More than a process, it is an experience. Too many individuals make decisions based on their accumulated experiences; others make them on the best of current knowledge and research. All that is fine, even desirable. However, leaders of hope base decisions on the vision of God's plan for humanity, and they learn of that in reflection, meditation, and contemplation.

Five Suggestions

1. Make judgments you can live with and die with.
2. Train yourself to leave aside prejudice in decision making.

3. Learn a simple method of meditation; if necessary, find a teacher.
4. Think of the consequences in others' lives of what you do.
5. Besides preparing yourself with research and analysis for your work as a leader, also ready your heart and soul.

4. ASK QUESTIONS NO ONE ELSE DOES

Leadership deals with establishing the vision of hope in our contemporary human communities. This means going beyond what leaders have done in the past. It means struggling with more fundamental questions, living in a state of sustained dissatisfaction with what has been achieved, looking to the future in hope, and being willing to live with the tensions of human frailty in its search for the best human values and for God. All this will mean new ways of looking at the world, new experiments in community interaction, and new percolating structures. Leadership questions today are philosophical and theological. How does what I do affect the human community? How do my decisions reflect God's plan for humanity? Am I maturing as a human being through my leadership? Am I aware of my covenant with the organization I serve and of the organization's covenant with its customers, shareholders, and so on? Do I serve the common good? Do my colleagues and I reflect the best of humanity? Does my leadership image the past or explore the future? "Some executives answer questions that arise. Others identify questions that need answers. Others come up with the answers before anyone knows the questions."[9]

When a leader of hope makes decisions, he or she should ask, why am I doing this, not only in the short term but in the long term too? In later life will I be proud of what I do today? Am I exploring enough? Who will be affected by what I do and how? Can I live with the impact my decisions will have on people? Is my decision not only good for the firm and its shareholders, but also for the workers, their families, and this community? As I make a decision would my spouse or closest friends be proud of what I am doing? Would a mentor or someone I have always looked up to take pride in knowing he or she contributed to what I do?

Leaders of hope ask themselves if they are anticipating the future for which they long. If there are hurdles, can they jump over them? Can they find potentialities for good in the negativity they face? Sometimes it will simply mean reframing the issues; other times it will necessitate a questioning of stereotypical reactions. Then the questions must focus proactively on alternatives for the future beyond current trends and probable outcomes; questions that do not imply looking to the future from here but looking to the present from a believed-in future. What are the alternatives that we can use to achieve our goals equally well but that do more good?

Looking with foresight at the many opportunities ahead, leaders will need to be courageous and venturesome. When they recognize a window of opportunity that "may be opening and closing more rapidly than at any other time,"[10] they should ask, for what is this truly an opportunity? Looking to the future never means abandoning the past. Jesus said a wise leader knows how to bring out of his or her treasure house things both new and old.[11] These are wise leaders who "plunge wholeheartedly into unfamiliar depths," transform situations, "turning the status quo into something special," and they tie a familiar past with a new reality.[12] The leader of hope constantly asks, is what I do in keeping with the best of who we are as human beings?

Five Suggestions

1. Question yourself on the reasons for your decisions.
2. Do not offer answers until you have exhausted the questions.
3. See yourself and encourage others to see you as a person who asks questions, not as someone who gives answers.

4. Ask questions about the future, not the past.

5. Ask beyond and beneath what others ask.

5. TEACH A NEW UNDERSTANDING OF COMMITMENT

Every good leader challenges self and followers to wholehearted commitment. The leader of hope links professional commitment to the integral human, spiritual maturing of self and each follower. Professional commitment becomes part of one's spirituality and thus draws out discretionary dedication from everyone. In this context, outstanding performance is a matter of personal growth, integrity, character development, and simply being who one feels called to be. Leaders must fire followers' hearts to see professional dedication and spirituality as two facets of the same life.

Leaders enthuse followers to be dedicated to a shared vision of hope. Commitment relates to the future and so includes imagination, contemplation, and hope. This implies networking to discover other people's hopes and constantly urging and encouraging others to be open to the unexpected. Commitment is essentially making the vision of hope real in the present.

This commitment to hope implies transformative action as part of one's dedication. Leaders of hope not only have a deep capacity for hope, but a lifelong dedication to realizing the future we long for. Doing well needs to be permeated by doing good; ethics matters in one's commitment. This includes strengthening the conviction that work leads to transformation. The primary commitment of a leader is personal transformation; all else follows from this focus.[13]

Commitment is relational. Others are included in our commitment and we are in theirs. It means sharing experiences, integrating individual and communal dedication to shared goals—professional and personal. This calls for mutual trust, benevolence toward each other, and shared hope. It implies mutual dedication to draw out the best in everyone and to capitalize on the unique contribution each one can make.

There must be a commitment to each other to work synergetically. Synergy "means working together of unlike elements to create desirable results greater than the independent parts can do."[14] No one can achieve significant transformation alone. Individual commitment is everyone's business. This "fusion leadership" makes productivity and professional development a part of personal and communal spirituality. "Fusion is about joining, coming together, creating connections and partnerships. It is about reducing barriers by encouraging conversations, information sharing, and joint responsibility across boundaries."[15]

Commitment means encouraging each other to be leaders. No one can be passive, for we live in a time of great need for quality leadership.[16] Everyone needs to be inspired but also to inspire, to be motivated but also to motivate, to be healed but also to heal, to be taught but also to teach, and to be led but also to lead. This commitment to mutual leadership implies humility, listening, mutual appreciation, and a sense of group development.

Commitment not only implies excellence, hope, transformative action, sharing, fusion, and mutual leadership, but it calls for selfless, loving service at every level of the organization. Leaders can no longer hide from major trends in contemporary society or become faceless to the social needs for justice and equality. In practice this means that one's commitment includes daily striving to understand others, to share with them and receive emotional support, and to show care and mutual compassion. This loving service will also manifest quality commitment in collaboration in culturally and gender-diverse situations. For a leader of hope, commitment is not merely to a job well done, but to a vision of community.

Five Suggestions

1. Think about ways you can make an ideal future alive today.
2. Ask yourself why you are committed at work and what the quality of your commitment is.
3. Check how you contribute to the development of your colleagues.
4. If you contribute more on your own than with others, ask why.
5. Identify the links between your professional dedication and personal spirituality.

6. UNLOCK THE POTENTIALS OF THE HEART

The ideal human community is characterized by love. When people know they are loved, they respond with dedication and give their best. If a leader treats followers negatively, he or she will receive diminishing returns from followers. A good leader of hope shows everyone respect, and they know he or she speaks from the heart. Followers must find trust, honesty, and integrity in their leaders, and leaders must show respect for the dignity and competence of followers by trusting them, empowering them, providing significant responsibilities, giving teams authority, searching for consensus, providing an enjoyable working environment, establishing participative structures, and sharing power. Caring needs to be practical; the leader treats others with politeness, gentleness, candor, graciousness, and sensitivity. A good leader appreciates people, and they know it.

There is a tendency to underestimate the importance of affective and emotional aspects of leadership. But "openness to emotion expands significantly a leader's understanding of people."[17] Followers need to know that a leader is there for them. The leader must make sure that coworkers know they are not only respected, but also loved. Love includes deep understanding, sharing of ideas, sharing deeply personal feelings, giving and receiving emotional support, growing through relationships, giving help to each other, showing mutual need, and sharing affection.[18] Love is practical: "We need to give each other space so that we may both give and receive such beautiful things as ideas, openness, dignity, joy, healing, and inclusion. And in giving each other the gift of space, we need also to offer the gifts of grace and beauty to which each of us is entitled."[19] A great prophet summed up the challenges of a leader: "God asks of you, only this, to act justly, to love tenderly, and to walk humbly with your God" (Mic 6:8).

Jesus called his followers "disciples" until toward the end of his ministry when he said, "I do not call you servants any longer....but I have called you friends" (John 15:15). The evangelist said, "Having loved his own who were in the world, he loved them to the end" (John 13:1). Nowadays we are all followers, seekers, and friends. This calls for a new kind of communication and a new spirit of community. The mystery of contemporary hope-filled leadership is that it requires real friendship, love, and community among people who work together. The leader develops a vision of a loving community in which all strive for reciprocity, unity, and consensus. A leader of hope manages with "the wisdom of love."[20] Community also includes the practical steps of peacemaking; removing the negativity, gossiping, jealousy, and mutually destructive attitudes and behaviors, which are frequently found in immature organizations.

It is important that we all do everything with loving commitment for each other, the firm, customers, and stakeholders. We compete with others with fairness and justice. We provide customers with the best possible product or service we can. We work with colleagues and always enable them to reach their own potential. To all we strive to provide supportive, working relationships, mutual dialogue, collaboration, and persevering love. This spirit of community is not closed in on itself; rather, leaders reach out to local and regional communities with projects for the common good, for the needy, for wider community enrichment.

Five Suggestions

1. Examine your relationships with your workers and ask yourself if they like you.
2. Be sure that when people leave your presence they know they are loved.
3. Act justly, love tenderly, and walk humbly with your God.
4. Review with your workers whether the working environment is enjoyable.
5. Think of new ways to show your trust to those with whom you work.

7. CREATE INTERRUPTIONS

Our world of leadership seems sure of itself. Programs turn out graduates with a packet of skills to become leaders themselves. Well-known presidents and CEOs write their memoirs and tell us how it is done. Leadership centers share their secrets, and the workshop circuit is clogged up with every conceivable idea about leadership. Studying for an MBA or similar degree in other disciplines, graduating, and getting a good-paying job is not necessarily a major contribution to the field of leadership. Graduates might just be more of the same old approach that we need to get rid of. One of the good practices of a great leader is to interrupt this confident discourse. Pressing the pause button when everything seems to be moving smoothly takes courage. Leadership programs are not producing the hoped-for transformation, and learning from others can be a shocking experience. Often individuals who want to be good leaders must first unlearn much of what they have been taught. We have seen so many failures, and each leader inflicts his or her own particular damage. In this process of interruption, doubt and uncertainty are good points of departure, followed by a healthy suspicion and skepticism, and culminating in enjoying a little insecurity for a while.[21]

Part of the task of a great leader is to fight against the nearsightedness of contemporary leadership, to oppose the prepackaged answers, and to seek something deeper. This can be an anxious time for a leader. "Learning occurs between a fear and a need. On the one hand, we feel the need to change if we are to accomplish our goals. On the other hand, we feel the anxiety of facing the unknown and unfamiliar."[22] This frequently leads to criticism that is hard both to accept and to give in constructive ways, but it can lead to significant systemic change, especially among those who know the system well and are humble enough to accept its failures and deal with them.[23]

Often this questioning of the direction of leadership leads to conflict, but this too can raise the energy level and produce significant discussion. Conflict itself can lead to crisis that is an opportunity to make different judgments on the matters at hand. Even when interruptions lead to anger, leaders should still move ahead. Anger is good and healthy when it manifests the fight over views that are significant. No mature person gets angry over irrelevancies. Too many are apathetic even though they are well aware that changes are needed.

While interrupting the discourse on the nature of leadership, the leader can engage in networking to surface ideas that can lead to new directions. What a leader needs to do is stop people from telling the same old stories about leadership's successes and urge them to start narrating the right stories. All can reflect on their mistakes and some good they perceived in failures, or reflect on their successes and some of the problems they caused.

A lot of contemporary leadership is moderate management sprinkled with a little inspiration. If there is a culture of trust and a climate of creativity, then proactive individuals can think differently about the same things, engage in provisional thinking and decision making, and courageously move to explore new concepts about leadership at the margins of organizational life. Here the skills are flexibility, improvisation, alternative thinking, bypassing of problems, innovation, and breakthrough.

Five Suggestions

1. Spend some time reflecting on what is working in your leadership and what is not.
2. Identify those aspects of your leadership you would like to eliminate.
3. Think about which leadership practices in your organization you would like to stop.
4. Reflect on the leader you admire and ask yourself why.
5. Make sure you have created a climate where other people can interrupt your leadership.

8. MOTIVATE PEOPLE TO MOTIVATE THEMSELVES

Leading is essentially a matter of motivation; keeping oneself motivated through the ups and downs of work, and motivating followers toward an excellence that leads to their growth and maturing as well as greater efficiency. People have lots of energy, and when a leader catches it and channels it, great things can be achieved together. Without a leader's inspiration and persuasion, followers' gifts are log jammed, and their creative contributions go nowhere. A leader creates a suitable climate for the growth of ideas, fosters responsiveness and cooperation, and provides the creative spark that moves people forward. Great leaders of hope ask people to be greater than they are, and they work so that they might be.

A common error of leadership is to presume that motivation already exists because people come to work and put in their time. This mistaken assumption fails to appreciate that enthusiasm and apathy are two points on the same continuum. A person is motivated to one side or drifts to the other. A leader will demonstrate his or her trust of others, encourage their self-confidence, maintain mature relationships with them, coach and guide them, model the way, inspire commitment, criticize constructively, and generate enthusiasm.[24] "If a leader has the will to develop people, there is no great mystery in how to do it...Bring them in on decisions. Delegate. Feed them responsibility. Stretch them. And change their assignments periodically."[25] Then we can add leave them alone.

In motivating others, leaders at times need to restrain their leadership, allowing followers to move alongside them. A leader should inspire, not order; pull, not push; and let people use their own initiative. Working alongside, a leader can ask probing questions, challenge expectations, affirm and reward successes, network, and build confidence through agreement.

In motivating others, a leader must involve them in the work at hand and the process of change. A leader of hope will delegate significant responsibilities, for this involves not only approval but an acceptance that affirms another's worth. In this way a good leader draws out the best in others and presents a vision that consists of making conscious what already lies unconscious in followers. When followers see the vision, they recognize it as their own and see how it fulfills their own hopes.

A leader of hope appreciates the advantages of surprise. A leader can surprise followers with anticipatory benevolence, an attitude of always anticipating good will toward others. In contemporary working environments, this surprising attitude of good will and affection can achieve wonders. Of course a good leader can also genuinely express happiness at being surprised at followers' achievements beyond expectations. Together leader and followers can surprise their customers with something beyond expectations, and surprise the local community with dedication no one thought possible. Research shows that satisfied workers or customers tell no one, but surprised workers and customers cannot stop telling others of their experiences.

Part of motivation is to foster a collective commitment to a vision of hope. People are liberated by hope and move forward with excitement. People who are motivated and filled with hope are generous, joyful, peaceful, and more productive—individually and communally.

Five Suggestions

1. Identify ways to keep yourself motivated in your work.
2. List the ways you try to motivate others.
3. Train yourself to get out of the way and let others find their own leadership.
4. Involve workers in significant responsibilities.
5. Think of ways to surprise your workers and customers.

These good practices of a leader of hope relate closely to each other. Some are easier to develop than others. Working at one or two will also increase appreciation of the others. Leaders of hope may well focus on other practices in addition to these, such as living with the memory of suffering, peacemaking, planning in hope, or working at the margins. The key conclusion is that today's leaders need the usual managerial and leadership skills, but these must be complemented with a series of attitudes and practices that manifest commitment to a vision of hope.

CHAPTER EIGHT

HOPE'S STRATEGIES

THE leader of hope has a different understanding of the call to leadership than other leaders. He or she appreciates a changed view of a leader's purpose in life, a new sense of destiny, and creative insights into the nature of leadership. Such a leader is prophetical, mystical, charismatic, and healing, and models a series of good practices that manifest a commitment to a vision of hope. This leadership begins with a personal transformation, but it cannot stop there. Leadership belongs to a community and involves the participation of all.

Leaders of hope create new forms and structures for a new kind of organization. Many leaders have lost their way and lost their values. "We believe that to regain our balance we must create alternative ways of working and living together. We need to invent a new, more meaningful model for business, education, health care, government, and family."[1] Leadership becomes a cooperative endeavor; we must imagine our organizations in new forms. Many in power make their own past normative, but no organization, not even religion with its particular claims, has an unchanging structure. New ways of structuring organizations are inventible, based on the vision of hope for all of humanity.

1. THE HOPEFUL ORGANIZATION

An individual who has experienced the transformative conversion that leads to spiritual leadership knows we must change the values on which we base our society's structures. Changing ourselves is not enough; we must change the system and institutionalize the vision of hope. "If we change our attitudes, our habits, and the ways of some of our institutions, it can be an age of new discovery, new enlightenment, and new freedoms—an age of true learning."[2] There is no reason why our organizations cannot be self-generating, liberating, healing, and hope-filled as well as being competitive, innovative, and successful. A leader of hope constantly searches for the connection between doing a good job in the present and being faithful to the vision of promise. The life of a lonely leader of hope is shortlived unless he or she can design a system that is faithful to the values and vision of hope. This means putting in place basic common values, a common enduring purpose, a community vision, and a shared mission in hope. "What is needed is fundamental transformation in the foundation (the roots) of the organization. Until that foundation is transformed into one with more justice, dignity, service, trustworthiness, and love, all the strategies, slogans, and training programs in the world will not help."[3]

Many leaders today are afraid of the future and so cling to non-essentials; they are paralyzed by the existing order and do not know how to get out of it; they are oppressed by workers' lack of loyalty, the existence of extremes, low morale, secrecy, pervasive doubt, and insecurity. Leaders who engage in a fundamental transformation of the organization will need to create a positive climate in which everyone feels mutually responsible and dedicated to the long-term transformation of the organization.[4] This redefining of the links between everyone in the organization is a first step toward structural change.[5]

In working with others to institutionalize the vision of hope, a leader will need a new set of instincts about leadership, instincts that at first seem unnatural but are part of the wisdom contemporary leaders need.[6] One author presents six of these new instincts, or what he calls core values:

1. Being faithful is more important than being successful.
2. Corporations should appreciate that they have a redemptive purpose.

3. Members need to be vulnerable to each other.
4. Belonging to an organization means being willing to take risks.
5. Belonging to a community requires intimacy.
6. We all need to be learners together.[7]

Another writer felt that a leader of an ideal community should work for:

1. One common standard: principle-centered goodness.
2. One heart: vision and direction.
3. One mind: purpose, mission, unity, and oneness.
4. One economic equality: no poor among them.[8]

I believe that in addition to the leader's basic instincts for the successful development of an organization of hope, he or she should make sure the organization has collegial government; stresses mission and values; administers collaboratively; practices subsidiarity; encourages self-managed teams; builds community; shows special appreciation for all workers; fosters an open and trusting culture; and encourages continuing education.[9] "The true test of an organization is the presence of a spirit of performance. An organization that is high in spirit builds on and develops the strength of each person, and this results in common people doing extraordinary things."[10]

Many leadership strategies evidence a common failure. "We fail to understand that what we are seeking to change is alive. Instead we see our organizations as if they were machines."[11] We are self-designing people in community, and we can change our structural realities. However, we must respect the psychological stages of community development, just as we do of individuals. Any mature organization has three essential components: relationships, common task, and interaction between these two. No one will belong to a group unless individuals see that the group realizes common hopes, satisfies basic needs, and shares core values. The community then moves through five stages in its own living and life-giving development.

1. People of like mind come together.
2. They work to build a sense of solidarity.
3. They mature a shared vision.
4. They consolidate the organization's vision.
5. They focus on ongoing renewal.

Stages two, three, and five end with crises that lead to failure or break-throughs to new levels of growth.[12]

There are always complex tradeoffs in the development of organizations that seek shared life and values. Understanding them enables a leader to create a new innovative structure. Leaders must know what they want and work hard to get it. It is difficult but it is essential for the future. We have so many visionless organizations that destroy people's lives; we have so many leaders and followers whose hardness of heart kills an organization; we also see individuals working hard to restore life to organizations that should be left to die; and we also see several defunct, extinct organizations that were innovative, but it was not enough. Building an organization with a hope-filled vision is not only part of a leader's personal spiritual growth, but a gift to contemporary society.

Organizational restructuring is a collaborative endeavor. In this journey of Spirit there must be profound mutual appreciation; everyone must be confident that who they are and what they do will be respected. Each person should feel a sense of belonging, a conviction that each one is essential to the organization, and mutual expectations are clear. Each one has significant competencies, knows one's own role, and feels a sense of obligation to each person. All members will need a capacity for authentic interpersonal relations, should together build an inspiring environment, and should be practical in establishing helpful evaluations and specific ways of solving disagreements. The community exists when people experience themselves striving together to realize the reason why they freely came together in the first place.

People can respond to almost any challenge provided they are given support and the leadership they need to use their talents effectively. The role of the leader is to create an environment in which everyone can grow naturally. He or she creates a new sense of responsibility, mutuality, honesty regarding hopes, and accountability. The more a leader has a healthy sense of self, the more he or she can believe in the worth of others. In fact, collaborating in changing structures requires humility to realize just how much a leader needs to work with others and value their gifts. The leader relentlessly emphasizes mission and values, hires carefully with common values in mind, creates collaborative structures at all levels, insists on a spirit of dialogue, fosters innovative thinking, establishes a culture of ongoing learning, and maintains a sense of awe, wonder, and mystery.[13] The leader reverences others, their gifts, and the common future for which they strive. "We believe a learning organization must be grounded in three foundations: 1. a culture based on transcendent human values of love, wonder, humility, and compassion; 2. a set of practices for generative conversation and coordinating action; and 3. a capacity to see and work with the flow of life as a system."[14]

In the task of establishing and maintaining a structure of hope, followers' roles include an attitude of being a member of the community, a capacity for authentic interpersonal relationships, and reasonable maturity. They, too, need clear ideas about what they want and how they envision the organization's future. Followers need to be dedicated to each other, to be clear regarding mutual expectations, and to be accepting of the competencies of others. Of course, followers should be respectful of others' dignity, protecting their reputation, privacy, security, freedom of expression, the right to speak and be heard, and so on. They also need to consciously empower the leader and to risk trusting his or her decisions.[15]

2. PLANNING WITH HOPE

The essential task of leadership, which is a teaching one, is to plan for and implement change. If leaders do not change and renew their organizations, obsolescence appears and death is inevitable. Some planning by objectives and long-range planning simply extend the present into the future. This kind of planning "does not deal with future decisions. It deals with the futurity of present decisions."[16] Several leadership scholars now speak about "the future of leadership," and urge leaders to "focus in on innovation." For these writers the task of leaders must include "envisioning the future," looking to the future, "thinking in the future tense," "leading for innovation," and establishing "visionary thinking and breakthrough leadership." They urge leaders to develop intellectual curiosity, a feel for patterns, "letting ourselves play, dream, and rest," "courageous patience," and a restless pursuit of what lies ahead.[17]

The challenge of envisioning the future is the responsibility of the leader of hope. Employees can help establish and implement a vision, but envisioning a different social order is the work of a leader; the hope-filled leader sees something that others do not. Over a quarter century ago, we heard the challenge, "We have to release this death grip on the past and deal with the future."[18] Unfortunately, even now, few have the skills. Envisioning the future is not forecasting, nor long-range planning, nor incremental change, nor an extension of the past. We seek an organization that focuses on the future and has the courage to confront the unknown. Leading to the future must be a way of life for leader and followers, all contributing to the vision that will give hope.

The future is open to a variety of possibilities, and many approaches will mold and form our organizations. However, the very openness of the future is an invitation and a challenge to create a reality that we would experience as satisfying on both an individual and a communal level. The usual method of planning is from the present to the future. The leader of hope attempts to look at the present from the future perspective. Thus, our concrete planning is more influenced by the created future and the vision of promise, and the leader take steps from that perspective. This approach to planning is filled with hope as well as a belief in transformation and change.

1. The process begins with a candid analysis of the present situation in which we find ourselves as an organization. How do we realistically see ourselves in regard to our life, mission, purpose, and effectiveness? How do others see us? What are our strengths and what are the areas that need further development? When we have adequately identified our present reality, we leave it aside for a while.

2. Envisioning a desirable future for an organization based on the vision of promise is challenging because it calls forth the potential and the vision that is often stifled within individuals and within groups. Placing ourselves in the future, with the problems and realities of the present blotted out, enables us to create an ideal image of what we would like our organization to be. While this might be a "leap into the unknown" regarding product development, new services, new niche, and so on, leaders do not enter the unknown regarding matters of justice, equality, community, service, mutuality, and so on, for they are known components of God's plan for humanity. Leaders of hope focus on visioning organizations that emphasize humanity, human rights, human development, and the future of humanity. "We are now entering an Age of Unreason, when the future, in so many areas, is there to be shaped by us and for us—a time...for bold imagining in private life as well as public, for thinking the unlikely and doing the unreasonable."[19] In this phase we consider all aspects of life and sharing, and the ideal of the group is presumed to be a reality. Leaders must challenge followers, convincing them that what seems impossible is not.

3. Following these two steps, the leader confronts the ideal hoped for with the present reality as already described. The comparison challenges leaders and followers to identify the areas that need to be changed in order to attain the ideal, and to call individuals to act together and not give up. As individuals and as a group, the participants see areas of

needed healing and transformation; they confront their ideal future with God's vision of hope. This reflective stage deepens insights and commitment, and clarifies obstacles and potentialities.

4. The planning stage begins with the ideal image or goal of the group. The leader encourages all members to have active, involved, optimistic, urgent, determinative approaches to this future. The leader and the organization embody this long-term goal in a series of attainable objectives. Presuming the goals are attained in, let us say, five years, the group plans backward to the present. This "long term backward path to the future"[20] requires "discontinuous upside-down thinking to deal with it, even if both thinkers and thoughts appear absurd at first sight."[21] The planning is from the presumed future backward to the present, thus bringing the future into reality. These goals need to be specific, which is the result of participation.

5. However, planning needs more than objectives; it also requires implementation. This is where many groups fail, often because of a lack of a shared commitment or some individuals' resistance to anything new.[22] The group also plans the appropriate action items, the steps they need to take in order to make the ideal a reality within a given period of time. Implementing the ideal is not the work of a few, but the responsibilities of each member of the group. The community asks itself the following questions: What are we to do? Who is to do it? When are we to do it? Where do we do it? How? Why? The result is a workable plan that is the creation of the participants and based on a future vision of hope.

There are many advantages in using this approach to planning. It integrates psychological and spiritual realities, sociological and faith dimensions of life. It involves the participants on levels of sharing and dialogue, so that the very qualities that are needed to make the ideal a reality are exercised and developed in the process. This work is a Christian hope-filled one that integrates content, sharing, and reflection; the process itself educates. Prayer and discernment, more than technique, are the backbone of the process. In a practical way, the problems of the present do not bog us down, nor does the heaviness of administration. The future can be different if we want it to be. If the plan is seen to be ideal but attainable, it will compel people to perform beyond normal levels.

The key to the effectiveness of the process is ongoing evaluation, and a good leader builds this into the planning. Hope is always ahead; when you get close to attaining your goals, develop new ones. The planning is an exciting, relaxed, and practical approach to help us move creatively and effectively into the future we desire.

3. SIGNS OF A HOPEFUL ORGANIZATION

1. Openness

A hopeful organization is one that is essentially open to the future in hope. This implies its members are always willing to listen and to learn, for they are willing to learn from others and be enriched by them. Being open to the gift of the future means being open to transcendence, to transformation, and to the challenge of the vision of promise. This openness to the transforming future has practical consequences. It means welcoming change, accepting the correction and challenge of others, valuing diversity—racial, religious, traditional, cultural, linguistic, and educational. All this leads to a free movement of information, open communication without secrecy, a readiness to question others' assumptions and to being questioned by others. In these ways members of an organization prepare themselves to welcome new ideas, to identify the gifts of others, and to rejoice in their goodness.

To attain adequate openness for a hopeful organization means establishing open institutional structures, and that means accepting disagreement and even dissent—not tolerating such reactions but recognizing that they are part of our openness and discovery of a shared future of hope. Openness means humbly acknowledging one's insufficiency, appreciating the importance of community, heralding the enrichment that comes through others, and preparing for the vision of promise.

2. *Collaboration and Dialogue*

Collaboration is not a way of doing something more efficiently, but a way of being an organization of hope more authentically. It is a communal expression of the shared values of the institution. Collaboration requires the friendship of faith, where love and mutual respect manifest the conviction that we are incomplete without each other. It requires love, humility, interior freedom, selflessness, a desire to seek the truth, and a commitment to serve the common good. It is enhanced by simple human qualities of truthfulness, gentleness, respectful listening, and mutual encouragement. It fosters harmony in plurality, diversity and dissent, reciprocal openness, sensitivity to new ideas, enhancement of communal sharing, and attentiveness to the input of others.

In genuine collaboration we experience peace of soul, freedom of spirit, detachment from our own ideas. There is an ease of dialogue, an acceptance of discerned truth, and courageous fidelity to build the future together. This kind of collaboration results in a practical expression of shared convictions in hope. It is more than advice or consultation, for it implies that members respect the group and that all take responsibility and initiative in pursuing common goals and in decision making. In a collaborative environment, members do not look for winners and losers, but rather seek to optimize everyone's contributions. It is a genuine form of shared authority that seeks truth, shares love, serves the common good, and leads to stability of shared values.

3. *Freedom*

A leader of hope guarantees freedom to followers, freedom to be who they want to be and say what they want to say. People who are afraid to challenge, to criticize, or to speak out can never contribute what the organization needs from them. Leaders of hope leave individuals free to make the decisions they are capable of making, rather than arrogantly centering all decision making on themselves. A great leader is not attached to his or her own leadership but utilizes subsidiarity and delegation whenever possible.

Freedom also includes confrontation, anger, and even a little violence from the rebellious in the group, but a good leader knows to listen attentively. "But to be free, people have to be freed. They have to be freed from fears that inhibit them; they have to be freed from prejudice and false information that keeps them from making proper decisions; they have to be freed from the ruts in which they are stuck through years of acting unreflectively; they have to be freed from apathy and dullness; they have to be freed from a certain amount of sin that has drifted into their lives."[23] A leader of hope not only grants freedom to followers, but also enables it in them.

4. Value Centered

A hopeful organization centers its life and development on a series of core values. These are basic values that the organization has agreed will motivate it in its internal life and in its service to the community. These values come from the founding and evolving mission. Some will be perennial, but others will change over time, as situations differ and as new members enrich the original mission with fresh insights. Members of an organization need to root their values in the original vision, interpret them for changing times, and then discover new ways to enrich the original vision. Members must reflect these core values in their own core expertise and talents, and all new employees hired need to dedicate themselves faithfully to these shared values.

Together the members of the organization should be aware of their distinctive contribution, be able to articulate their group's values, and have a pervading passion for the organization's shared mission. One's personal values should match the organization's values; these together form the organization's enduring purpose—the very reason for its existence, and these together should be the values of the future. Thus these values are the basis for the mission of the organization and should be implemented in a strategic vision.

5. *A Sense of Mystery and Awe*

A hopeful organization looks to the future to which God calls us. This vision of who we can be and ought to be requires that individuals be reflective and contemplative so that their minds and hearts are ready to receive the call that comes with this vision. Leaders and followers alike need to be still, quiet, and receptive to the call of the future. They need to train themselves to be inspired by the wonders of daily life so that they can appreciate the beauty of the vision of hope. They have to be people who can concentrate on the simple events of daily life so that they can enjoy and savor the goodness of their calling to be an organization of hope. Finally, they cannot be individuals whose lives are cluttered with the trivia of modern life, but must be people who can be silent and appreciative of the dimensions of loving community to which their organization can contribute.

A hopeful organization lives in an environment of gratitude, awe, and mystery. They know they are part of something wonderful. This spirit of mystery and awe not only refers to the organization's future, but to every member in the group with his or her wonderful gifts, to the leader and his or her dedicated service, to the stakeholders and their support, and to the surrounding community and its needs that the organization seeks to meet.

6. *Love*

Without creating a sense of mutual appreciation and love, an organization will always be stunted in seeking its fullest development. "A loveless organization has selfishness, political infighting, petty jealousies, lies, and distrust."[24] When love becomes a distinctive feature of organizational development, then humility, trust, reconciliation, and mutual respect become aspects of everyday life. Love lets us treat people in light of hope; in light of what they can and will become, rather than who they are now. When we speak about a vision of hope, what we are actually longing for is a loving community. Genuine love of others within an organization is nurturing, strengthening, and hope filled. It begins with simple gestures of respect, concern, compassion, kindness, humility, gentleness, and patience. These basic expressions of community are humanizing, caring, trusting, and supportive. Love within an organization implies creative tolerance of ambiguity and differences, and it calls for mutual forgiveness, reconciliation, and peacemaking. When an organization commits itself to be a loving community, you can sense it, you can feel it.[25]

People who feel loved by those around them sense interdependence and solidarity with them, can more easily strive together for common goals, and even feel friendship for each other. Mutual love leads to inspiration, courage, and vitality. The group's meetings and discussions reflect this reality. A loving community does not happen by chance, but as a result of the deliberate shift of focus from self to others. The leader of hope has faith in others, engages them honestly, supports them enthusiastically, shares deeply with them, and constantly strives to make a difference in their lives. "People decisions—selection, rewards, and promotion—are the true control of an organization. People decisions direct behavior because they indicate the actual values in action of the organization."[26]

7. Creativity

Creativity is an expression of something deep within us that we have never expressed before. It could be a new understanding of the organization's mission, or a new interpretation of a spirit of service, a new style of decision making, or a new form of relationships. It is both an attitude and a process of an individual but also of a group that through collaboration, insight, artistic ability, and technological skill creates something together that each could never do alone. Creativity is linked to a discovery of a hope-filled vision of the future. When present in an organization, it makes people feel better about themselves by energizing and strengthening their self-concept. It is especially enriched in a workplace of diversity, innovative ideas, and nontraditional thinking. Some leaders think about their legacy, which means looking to their past achievements. Great leaders guide others to find their true selves in a future, creative vision. The leader disappears and the followers emerge.

Creativity and discovery are nurtured by continuing education, reflection, and sharing. Creativity implies a readiness to think differently, to act differently, and to be different; not to be confined by the present, but ready to discover and implement the future to which we feel called. Leaders and workers alike need unpressured time, opportunity to discern carefully, ability to critically assess alternatives, and a commitment to realize the future vision. A leader of hope makes this happen. This leads to new opportunities for synthesis, to see new relationships, to see connections and interrelationships that can bring insight, creative assessment, and openness to transcendent values.

8. Optimism

An organization of hope maintains a working environment of peace, where members can grow together spiritually in attaining the organization's mission. An organization of hope with hope-based leadership is life giving to itself and to its stakeholders. People enjoy working for such an organization and enthusiastically give themselves to each other and to their shared task. Optimism, enjoyment, and enthusiasm are three interconnected concepts in a hope-filled organization. Enthusiasm describes a person possessed by the values of God (*en theos*); it refers to someone who is guided by God and lives according to the vision of God. Joy is an essential component of Christian life, preceding and concluding every faith- and hope-filled action. "Serving the neighbor becomes an 'enjoyment,' one of the chief ends of human existence."[27]

Optimism is the attitude of one who takes a hopeful view of things, expects a positive outcome, and anticipates the good to which his or her commitment leads. When an organization is characterized by optimism, joy, and enthusiasm, it raises the level of satisfaction of all its members, it deepens their commitment to a common vision, and it leads to growth in relationships and love.

9. Resilience

Leaders of hope look to the future with confidence based on faith in the vision of promise. This is the reason for their hope. But there are many small tentative hopes that they explore as ways of implementing the vision of hope. These exploratory hopes sometimes come to nothing and when they do, the great vision of hope must remain. There will be many failures, but leaders and followers alike must not become discouraged. Rather, in ever changing circumstances, when the small hopes fail, they need to find new ones to achieve as part of the journey toward the realization of the vision. Their strategy must include incremental steps toward hope, constant evaluation to establish relevance, and careful analysis of followers' resistance to the new directions suggested. Adaptation needs to be fast, solutions are nearly always tentative, and recommitment to the process must be unyielding.

Leaders and followers can learn a lot from reflection on failures; they can clarify goals, refocus hopes, reassess community skills, reevaluate environment, and rejuvenate the organization's enduring purpose. Everyone needs to help in creating what the organization stands for. The ability to confront crises in the organization is an essential task of leadership. Crises give occasions to judge things from a different perspective and then move ahead with renewed confidence. Whether the crisis is a major turning point or a creeping daily crisis, leaders need to bounce back, reenergize the followers, and move on. It is all part of living in hope.

10. Outsider Mentality

Only a small percentage of leaders will be leaders of hope. This kind of leadership is not based only on knowledge, skills, techniques, attitudes, and experiences, but also on personal transformation, a sense of call and destiny, a willingness to give priority to spirituality, and a dedication to implement the vision of hope. Such leaders are few, but they are essential because we can all learn from them. They are different from the run-of-the-mill leaders or inspired managers that are common today. These leaders need courage to be outsiders, for their commitment to values distinguishes them from others. This is part of the prophetical vocation of a leader of hope.

Being an outsider requires a healthy self-esteem, confidence, competence, and lots of energy. It will mean confronting confusion, fear, and some oppression, for there will always be mediocre leaders who cannot and will not change. Leaders will need humility so as to avoid the arrogance and self-righteousness that come with being different. Part of this humility will be to value the good that can be discovered in everyone. Organizations need the courage to work with leaders of hope. These leaders must make difficult choices; they will be criticized for not being practical enough, but they must choose hope, for it has far-reaching effects on the organization. It is one thing to be value centered and therefore different, and quite another to be an organization that thinks of itself as set apart. Clearly, the members need to achieve whatever is the day-to-day business of the organization. The outsider mentality must accompany the organization's total involvement in ordinary everyday life with all the normal interactions with other organizations. Leaders of hope are different but an integral part of recovering and renewing contemporary leadership.

CONCLUSION

Awakening Others to Hope

1. THE RESPONSE OF HOPE

LEADERSHIP means hope before any other quality, for creating a better future is the essence of leadership. We need a new kind of leadership where leaders act intentionally as leaders of hope, dedicated to implementing the vision. It must be a form of spiritual leadership, where a leader is motivated by the values deep within his or her heart. The question is, where do these values come from? I believe they come from a vision of hope. The hope to which I refer is based on a faith-filled understanding of what is the ultimate vision and goal of humanity. This vision emphasizes community, mutuality, justice, integrity, personal and communal fulfillment, and attitudes that result from these convictions. Anything that violates these principles cannot be part of a leader's life.

Hope reveals who we are and who we are called to become; it deals with the meaning of life and what it means to be human, and thereby informs how we should deal with the present. It opens the heart of our leadership style to the God of promise. In this light, the goal of leadership is not just organizational success, but the transformation of humanity. This transformation begins at the grass-roots level and percolates up through the entire organization.[1] This task focuses on how a leader sees the relationship between the human spirit and the absolute end in God. In fact, hope challenges us to live in light of this future.

Some people are reluctant to invest in hope because they have been disappointed. Unfulfilled hopes happen, but when consistent, the situation is worse than having no hope. For a leader, everything in life is colored by hope—call, purpose, destiny, and vision of leadership. The leader of hope sees his or her own call as one of personal transformation and then also enabling others to live out their own call. This inevitably means seeing one's own purpose in life in a new way, for the leader of hope appreciates that he or she must look at life differently, seeking truth, spreading love, and creating community, as well as all the normal tasks of efficient organizational development. Hope is very practical, while always open to transcendent values. Hope is not just in God, it is also in ourselves. So we cannot sit back and wait, for there is a dynamic interaction between now and the vision of promise. Hope is a future good, arduous and difficult to obtain, but always possible.

In addition to being a competent leader, the leader of hope has four essential tasks on behalf of others—to be a prophet, a mystic, a charismatic, and a healer. These tasks focus on what ought to be the way we live in the present, on insights gained in personal and profound experiences of light and darkness, on an appreciation of the interrelatedness of all gifts within the community, and on the liberating, healing, and redemptive dimensions of leadership.

Hope modifies everything a leader does, and hopeful leaders influence all around them. It leads to new approaches to leadership, new leadership habits that become good practices of leading. These will overflow from the leader into the organization. Hope needs an organization that is learning, sharing, contemplative, change-ready, innovative, and creative. The leader must develop hopefulness in others and train them in the habits and practices of hope. He or she leads people to the future. Leaders of hope appreciate that the hope they seek is not a noun but a verb; it is an activity that influences all they do.

2. AWAKENING OTHERS TO HOPE

1. Trusting

Leadership is the awakening of others to their own call; it is essentially a task of enabling others to meet their future. Followers only trust leaders who know where they are going. This trust fosters a sense of responsibility, and without trust we breed antileaders. The trust we place in leaders is based on their competence, commitment, communication skills, and vision of community. It is never given freely, but only earned. It is a way of legitimizing a leader's position and vision. Likewise, a leader's trust of followers depends on real knowledge about them, their values, and their responses to changing situations.

Trust gives birth to peace and allows all involved to feel confident about themselves and others as they approach their expectations about the future, to accept the integrity and authentic challenges of a leader, to communicate honestly about significant issues, and to take risks with people—at times without evidence or proof of their views. The quality of trust in a group often determines effectiveness, since it frees individuals to be the best they feel they can be. So, trusting others is a key initial action in awakening others to hope. It lets everyone accept others' ideas and suggestions, and it is a foundation of collaboration and mutual empowerment.

2. Supporting

We are all responsible for each other as we approach a vision of hope. Leaders are people who can strengthen others by affirming them, lifting them up, appreciating their contributions, and giving legitimacy to all the good they do. Criticized privately, supported publicly, followers feel competent, their self-esteem grows, and they know they are loved. Supporting other workers not only builds a sense of community, it contributes to the organization's competitive edge.

131

Workers value being supported and when they are, they think highly of their leaders and work harder.

When leaders support followers, they are providing them with an apprenticeship in hope, for supported workers can look forward to the appreciation and success of their own dreams. If support is not just a management technique but rather comes from the heart, then it motivates others to intensify their commitment to the organization's shared values and goals. Every little gesture of support helps to awaken hope in followers.

3. Inspiring

Leaders need to sustain hope in their followers and do so by their modeling, by their enthusiasm, joy, and optimism, and by inspiring their followers. "To inspire" means to put a new spirit in people (in spirit) and is always linked to a better future. Inspiring leadership is based on vision, meaningful and honest communication, and the fact that people know they are loved. When one of these three is missing, it is unlikely that followers will be inspired to work for the future vision.

When inspiration is present, the results are powerful and transforming. Inspiration imparts increased energy, gives followers a sense of well-being, encourages their creativity, facilitates a sense of community and common cause, enables people to transcend themselves in the service of others, brings peace, enthusiasm, and clarity of judgment, and helps us welcome the future for which we strive.[2] Inspiring others brings out the very best in them and enables them to transcend the present—their own and others', and lets them focus on the shared future of hope.

4. Choosing

When I refer to choosing as a component of awakening others to hope, I do not mean the hundreds of simple choices and decisions a leader makes every day. Only a few daily decisions have impact on vision, mission, and shared values. Choosing as a component of hope means always choosing that which is the most difficult. Some decisions are very important, others are of moderate significance, and others are decisions that people ask leaders to make but that have no real significance one way or the other. Leaders of hope focus on those decisions that have overriding importance for the future.

If a leader makes the important decisions, the others will take care of themselves, and the leader can always ignore the third class. Unfortunately, many so-called leaders immerse themselves in secondary decision making and never take care of real issues. Even when they consider the hard choices, they make the easy decisions within the hard choices. When a firm needs to cut back, there arises a series of hard decisions. Leaders of hope will consider every worker's importance and struggle to come up with a decision that is filled with hope. A leader without hope can simply cut jobs with no concern for the consequences, in other words, make an easy decision within a hard choice.

5. Daring

A leader of hope is a person of courage and determination. Courage comes from the Latin word for "heart," and a leader today needs the courage to be motivated by values, to be himself or herself, to be part of a community, and to be great for the sake of others. A leader of hope knows that his or her decisions lead to hope or despair. Making critical decisions will involve risk and often will lead to disagreement. In focusing on the future, innovation will not be so much a single event but a way of life, not a way of thinking but a way of being in the world. Being always open to the future requires the daring of the prophet, the depth of conviction of the mystic, the giftedness of the charismatic, and the sensitivity of the healer.

The leader of hope dares to see his or her own role and leadership differently, imagines fulfilling the skills and expectations of followers, structures organizations to build on everyone's gifts, and makes decisions as if every person mattered. The leader of hope dares to capitalize on the gifts of everyone, builds a sense of community belonging that produces different ways of relating, and accepts, appreciates, and loves all the people with whom he or she relates. More than anything else, he or she leads with perseverance and courage, daring to believe that the future can become reality.

6. Empowering

Leaders of hope identify the gifts of others. Empowering does not mean giving people power that they did not previously have, but rather seeing their gifts and liberating them to use their gifts for the benefit of the whole organization. The leader of hope spends time discovering, appreciating, and assessing other people's gifts, drawing out their good qualities, affirming them, and making sure all members of the organization affirm each other's gifts. "Credible leaders are not afraid to liberate the leader in everyone. If everyone is a leader, then everyone is responsible for guiding the organization toward its future."[3] This process of empowering implies risk taking, flexibility, experimentation, innovation, and failure without reprimand. Empowering lets people see their own importance to the organization, encourages them to empower others, identifies the interconnectedness of all members, and awakens them to new possibilities within the shared vision of hope.

7. Delegating

A leader of hope is always ready to facilitate and welcome the birth of new leadership in former followers. Such a leader pushes autonomy and responsibility down to others so that decisions are always made at the lowest level possible within the organization. This practice of subsidiarity means that delegation is meaningful, and people feel they have something worthwhile to contribute. A leader of hope knows when it is appropriate to get out of the way of other people's gifts, initiative, and responsibility. If a leader wants to get the best out of all followers, then he or she must delegate significant authority that followers see as worthwhile, challenging, and an important contribution to the future of the organization. Hope's vision is one of cooperation, collaboration, mutuality, and community, and leaders of hope must construct this vision at all levels of the organization, and thus create something that will live on after their own departure.

8. Celebrating

Leaders of hope celebrate their people's successes, honoring their key achievements with public recognition. Celebrations should not be perfunctory, but neither do they need to be elaborate. They are means of conveying gratitude, affirmation, shared joy, and anticipated hope. Simple but genuine celebrative rituals can punctuate an organization's life and development, lifting people out of monotony and boredom, bringing people together in joy, reinforcing their shared values, enthusiastically indentifying their successes, and binding them together in love.

Celebrating may well relate to what has already been achieved but, more important still, it creates attitudes that motivate people to look to the future in hope with the conviction that leaders will always value their ideas, their work, and their roles in the organization's development. While celebrating looks to the past, it anticipates the future in hope.

The heart and essence of leadership is to move people to a better situation. This is why great leaders are always filled with hope, and fill others with enthusiasm born of hope. There is no great leadership without a vision of hope. Leaders who believe in humanity and have the will to work for its transformation know it is time to hope again.

They keep their feet on the ground with the skills and talents of management and leadership, but they have something more. They view everything with the eyes of hope, surrender their hearts to a vision of hope, and dedicate themselves to the hope-filled transformation of society. This is what leadership is all about.

NOTES

INTRODUCTION

1. James M. Kouzes and Barry Z. Posner, "Seven Lessons for Leading the Voyage to the Future," in *The Leader of the Future*, Frances Hesselbein, Marshall Goldsmith, and Richard Beckhard, eds. (San Francisco: Jossey-Bass, 1996), 100.

2. Fred Kofman, and Peter M. Senge, "Communities of Commitment: The Heart of Learning Organizations," *Organizational Dynamics* 21 (Autumn 1993): 9.

3. See Marshall Goldsmith, *What Got You Here Won't Get You There* (New York: Hyperion Books, 2007).

CHAPTER ONE

1. See Juan Alfaro, "Christian Hope and the Hopes of Mankind," *Concilium* 59 (1970): 59, where he quotes Ernst Bloch.

2. Alfaro, "Christian Hope," 60.

3. Alfaro, "Christian Hope," 60.

4. Jürgen Moltmann, *Theology of Hope* (San Francisco: Harper and Row, 1967), 20.

5. See Michael Scanlon, "Hope," in *New Dictionary of Theology*, Joseph Komonchak, Mary Collins, and Dermot A. Lane, eds. (Collegeville, MN: Liturgical Press, 1987), 493.

6. See Ferdinand Kerstiens, "Hope," in *Sacramentum Mundi*, vol. 3. Karl Rahner and others, eds. (London: Burns and Oates, 1968), 64.

7. Letty M. Russell, *Changing Contexts of Our Faith* (Philadelphia: Fortress Press, 1985), 32.

8. See Richard P. McBrien, *Church: The Continuing Quest* (New York: Newman Press, 1970), 14–21, where he describes five views of the end times: 1. consistent, consequent, futurist; 2. realized; 3. existentialist; 4. salvation history; 5. proleptic.

9. Jürgen Moltmann, "Theology as Eschatology," in *The Future of Hope*, Jürgen Moltmann and others, eds. (New York: Herder and Herder, 1970), 10.

10. John Downey, ed., *Love's Strategy: The Political Theology of Johann Baptist Metz* (Harrisburg, PA: Trinity Press International, 1999), 7.

11. Dermot A. Lane, *Keeping Hope Alive: Stirrings in Christian Theology* (New York: Paulist Press, 1996), 66.

12. Jürgen Moltmann, *In the End—the Beginning: The Life of Hope* (Minneapolis, MN: Fortress Press, 2004), 17.

13. Moltmann, *Theology of Hope*, 32.

14. See Monika Hellwig, "Hope," in *The New Dictionary of Catholic Spirituality*, Michael Downey, ed. (Collegeville, MN: Liturgical Press, 1993), 512.

15. Michael Demaison, "The Christian Utopia," *Concilium* 59 (1970): 55.

16. Vivian Boland, "Hope," in *Modern Catholic Encyclopedia*, Michael Glazier and Monika Hellwig, eds. (Collegeville, MN: Liturgical Press, 1994), 402.

17. Rowan A. Greer, *Christian Hope and Christian Life* (New York: Crossroad Publishing Co., 2001), 15.

18. Scanlon, "Hope," 497.

19. Moltmann, *Theology of Hope*, 33.

20. Alfaro, "Christian Hope," 61.

21. Richard McBrien, *Catholicism*, vol. II (Minneapolis, MN: Winston Press, 1980), 973.

22. Ferdinand Kersteins, "The Theology of Hope in Germany Today," *Concilium* 59 (1970): 110–11.

23. Moltmann, *Theology of Hope*, 21.

24. Downey, *Love's Strategy*, 1.

25. Downey, *Love's Strategy*, 2.

26. Moltmann, *Theology of Hope*, 25.

27. See Downey, *Love's Strategy*, 2.

28. John Downey, "The Future of Political Theology," *Horizons* 34, no. 2 (2007): 306.

29. Mary Pulley, *Losing Your Job—Reclaiming Your Spirit: Stories of Resilience, Renewal, and Hope* (San Francisco: Jossey-Bass, 1997), 149.

CHAPTER TWO

1. Peter Kostenbaum, *Leadership: The Inner Side of Greatness* (San Francisco: Jossey-Bass, 1991), 6.

2. See Robert K. Greenleaf, *Servant Leadership: A Journey into the Nature of Legitimate Power and Greatness* (New York: Paulist Press, 1977), 16: "For something great to happen, there must be a great dream. Behind every great achievement is a dreamer of great dreams."

3. See Harrison Owen, *The Spirit of Leadership: Liberating the Leader in Each of Us* (San Francisco: Berrett-Koehler, 1999).

4. See Stephen R. Covey, "Three Roles of the Leader in the New Paradigm," in *The Leader of the Future: New Visions, Strategies, and Practices for the Next Era*, Frances Hesselbein, Marshall Goldsmith, and Richard Beckhard, eds. (San Francisco: Jossey-Bass, 1996), 149–59. Covey comments: "The most effective leaders are, first, models of what I call principle-centered leadership....These principles are woven into the fabric of every civilized society and constitute the roots of every organization that has endured." He then lists fairness, service, equity, justice, integrity, honesty, and trust.

5. Donna J. Markam, *Spiritlinking Leadership: Working through Resistance to Organizational Change* (New York: Paulist Press, 1999), 8.

6. Covey, "Three Roles of the Leader in the New Paradigm," 152, 155.

7. Thomas E. Cronin, "Reflections on Leadership," in *Contemporary Issues in Leadership*, William E. Rosenbach and Robert L. Taylor, eds. (San Francisco: Westview Press, 1993), 21.

8. See Gary A. Yukl, *Leadership in Organizations* (Upper Saddle River, NJ: Prentice Hall, 1989), 210.

9. Koesterbaum, *Leadership*, 91.

10. Lane, *Keeping Hope Alive*, 61.

11. Robert K. Greenleaf, "The Leadership Crisis," *Humanitas* 14 (1978): 304.

12. Stephen C. Harper, *The Forward-Focused Organization: Visionary Thinking and Breakthrough Leadership to Create Your Company's Future* (New York: AMACOM, 2001), 84.

13. Arthur Shriberg, Carol Lloyd, David L. Shriberg, and Mary Lynn Williamson, *Practicing Leadership: Principles and Applications* (New York: John Wiley and Sons, 1997), 203.

14. Dag Hammerskold, *Markings* (New York: Knopf, 1964).

15. Max De Pree, *Leadership Is an Art* (Lansing, MI: Michigan State University Press, 1987), 56.

16. Lee G. Bolman and Terrence E. Deal, *Leading with Soul: An Uncommon Journey of Spirit* (San Francisco: Jossey-Bass, 1995), 35.

17. Markham, *Spiritlinking Leadership*, 41.

18. Harper, *The Forward-Focused Organization*, 81; see Jack Hawley, *Reawakening the Spirit in Work: The Power of Dharmic Management* (San Francisco: Berrett-Koehler, 1993), viii.

19. See Hawley, *Reawakening the Spirit in Work*, viii; Koestenbaum, *Leadership*, 5, 60, 123; Pulley, *Losing Your Job, Reclaiming Your Spirit*, 157.

20. Lee G. Bolman and Terrence E. Deal, *Wizard and the Warrior: Leading with Passion and Power* (San Francisco: Jossey-Bass, 2006), 1.

21. James M. Kouzes and Barry Z. Posner, *Credibility: How Leaders Gain and Lose It, Why People Demand It* (San Francisco: Jossey-Bass, 1993), 240.

22. Lane, *Keeping Hope Alive*, 65.

23. See Robert Golford and Anne Siebold Drapeau, *The Trusted Leader* (New York: The Free Press, 2002), 8–16, where they give ten benefits of a trusted leader: frees people, fuels passion, provides focus, fosters innovation, gives people the time to get it right, lowers costs, is contagious, helps recruit people who are on the right wavelength, helps retain great employees, and improves quality of work.

CHAPTER THREE

1. It is unfortunate that we generally think a prophet predicts the future, since this takes the heart out of his or her mission to the community. Sometimes religions look back over the teachings of a prophet and see that he or she seems to foretell something. However, these are generally statements of faith. It is not that the past proves the future, but rather that the future is rooted in the past. Some disciples even write about events that have already taken place and make it look as if their leader foretold them. This is called "prophecy *ex eventu*," a prophecy made after the event has already taken place. The basic meaning of the word "prophet" is "to speak on behalf of God," coming from the Greek *pro pheme*—"to speak on behalf of."

2. See Bolman and Deal, *The Wizard and the Warrior*.

3. The specific references to the challenges of each of the prophets are given here in order. Isa 42—53; Jer 22:13; Mal 3:5; Amos 8:5; Hos 12:8; Mic 2:1–10; 6:10; Ezek 45:9–12; Mic 3:11; Isa 1:23; 5:23; Jer 34:8–22; Amos 2:6-8; Isa 10:1–2; 3:15; Jer 5:26; Amos 2:6–8; 4:1; 5:7–13; Zech 7:9–12; Isa 3:1–2; Jer 5:4; Hos 2:18–22; Jer 31:31-34; Ezek 36:25–29.

4. The book of the prophet Isaiah is generally divided into three parts, each written by a different author: First Isaiah 1—39, Second Isaiah 40—55, and Third Isaiah 56—66.

5. See the following specific references. Jer 21:12b; Isa 1:17; Amos 5:10–15; Isa 58:10; Jer 22:17; Isa 58:6–7.

6. See Jer 7:4–7; Amos 8:5; Isa 1:15; Mic 6:8.

7. The title "prophet" is frequently attributed to Christ. Matt 13:57; 16:14; 21:11; Mark 6:4; 6:14–15; 8:28; Luke 4:24; 7:16, 39; 9:7–8; 13:33; 24:19; John 4:19, 44; 6:14; 7:40, 52; 9:17; Acts 3:22–23; 7:37.

8. Early Christian writings like the *Didache* speak of prophets in the early church as leaders of worship and as teachers.

9. *Dogmatic Constitution on the Church*, Vatican Council II, 35.

10. R. B. Y. Scott, *The Relevance of the Prophets* (New York: Macmillan, 1944), 151.

11. See Walter Brueggemann, *The Prophetic Imagination* (Minneapolis, MN: Fortress Press, 1987), 67.

12. Greenleaf, *Servant Leadership*, 8. It is not easy to agree on what constitutes a vision of hope or promise. There are at times several competing visions that nowadays are often based on taboos or forbidden positions—no this, no that, no the other. Some leaders have no hope-filled vision, since it is impossible to construct a future vision out of misplaced myopic thinking.

13. James M. Kouzes and Barry Z. Posner, *The Leadership Challenge: How to Get Extraordinary Things Done in Organizations* (San Francisco: Jossey-Bass, 1988), 102: "Visions, then, are conceptualizations. They're images in the mind, impressions and representations. They become real as leaders express those images in concrete terms to their constituents. Just as architects make drawings and engineers build models, leaders find ways of giving expression to their hopes for the future."

14. See Burt Nanus, *Visionary Leadership: Creating a Compelling Sense of Direction for Your Organization* (San Francisco: Jossey-Bass, 1992), 16. James Kouzes and Barry Z. Posner. "It's Not Just the Leader's Vision," in *The Leader of the Future 2: Visions, Strategies, and Practices for the Next Era*, Frances Hesselbein and Marshall Goldsmith, eds. (San Francisco: Jossey-Bass, 2006), 211: "Leaders really struggle with communicating an image of the future that draws others in. It's not that leaders don't have a personal conviction about the future or spend time thinking about it; it's just that they don't effectively speak to what others see and feel about it."

15. See Nanus, *Visionary Leadership*, 156.

16. Stephen Covey, *7 Habits of Highly Effective People: Restoring the Character Ethic* (New York: Simon and Schuster, 1989), lists the habits as the following: Be proactive; Begin with the end in mind; Put first things first; Think win/win; Seek first to understand then to be understood; Synergize; Sharpen the saw.

17. Warren Bennis and Burt Nanus, *Leaders* (New York: Harper and Row, 1985), 82.

18. See R. S. Khare and David Little, *Leadership* (University Press of America, 1984), 132: "Any leader has to move back and forth between some set of concepts and principles, goals and dreams that he may have, and the hard, grubby task of giving them form and shape. Somehow the leader must accept the fact that there are stubborn realities, moral realities for example that may require harsh decisions very often as well as gentle and supportive decisions."

19. See Charles Handy and Warren Bennis, *The Age of Unreason* (Boston: Harvard Business School Press, 1990), 72.

20. Bernard Häring, *A Theology of Protest* (New York: Farrar, Straus and Giroux, 1970), 112.

21. Shriberg and others, *Practicing Leadership*, 198.

22. The phrase "creating dangerously" comes from Camus, and Warren Bennis and Burt Nanus quote it in their book *Leaders*, 23.

23. See Paul Minear, *To Heal and to Reveal: The Prophetic Vision According to Luke* (New York: Seabury Press, 1976), 87, where he gives ten characteristics of a prophet.

24. Brueggemann, *The Prophetic Imagination*, 88.

25. Brueggemann, *The Prophetic Imagination*, 88.

26. Peter Senge refers to "massive failure of leadership foresight." See "Systems Citizenship: The Leadership Mandate for this Millennium," in *The Leader of the Future 2: New Visions, Strategies, and Practices for the Next Era*, Frances Hesselbein and Marshall Goldsmith, eds. (San Francisco: Jossey-Bass, 2006), 40.

27. Brueggemann, *The Prophetic Imagination*, 13.

28. See Brueggemann, *The Prophetic Imagination*, 45, 95.

29. Donald E. Messer, *Contemporary Images of Christian Ministry* (Nashville: Abingdon Press, 1989), 139. For references to Jesus' servant leadership, see Phil 2:7; Matt 20:25–28.

30. Leonard Doohan, *Spiritual Leadership: The Quest for Integrity* (New York/Mahwah, NJ: Paulist Press, 2007), 93–95.

CHAPTER FOUR

1. See Leonard Doohan, *Spiritual Leadership*, 106–20.

2. This is the subtitle of the book by Lee G. Bolman and Terrence E. Deal, *Leading with Soul: An Uncommon Journey of Spirit* (San Francisco: Jossey-Bass, 1995).

3. Kofman and Senge, "Communities of Commitment," 9.

4. Handy and Bennis, *The Age of Unreason*, 24.

5. Bolman and Deal, *The Wizard and the Warrior*, 21.

6. Hawley, *Reawakening the Spirit in Work*, 59.

7. See Leonard Doohan, *Spiritual Leadership*, chapter six, "Leadership and Reflection."

8. There are a series of television commercials on that parallel what happens in nature with leadership skills. This idea of creation as guru is an example of the new leadership learning.

9. Nancy J. Eggert, *Contemplative Leadership for Entrepreneurial Organizations* (Westport, CT: Quorum Books, 1998), 122–23. Eggert uses ideas from Meister Eckhart as interpreted by Matthew Fox.

10. See "The Dark Night," in *The Collected Works of St. John of the Cross*, translated by Kieran Kavanaugh, OCD, and Otilio Rodriguez, OCD (Washington, DC: ICS Publications, 1979).

11. See Leonard Doohan, *Spiritual Leadership*, 79–82.

12. Leland Kaiser, *The Road Ahead—Transform Yourself, Your Organization, and Your Community* (Englewood, CO: Estes Park Institute Notes, 1998), 126.

13. David A. Ramey, *Empowering Leaders* (Kansas City: Sheed and Ward, 1991), 94.

14. Hawley, *Reawakening the Spirit in Work*, 4.

15. John of the Cross, "Spiritual Canticle," v. 28.

CHAPTER FIVE

1. Bennis and Nanus, *Leaders*, 224: "Charisma is the result of effective leadership, not the other way around, and that those who are good at it are granted a certain amount of respect and even awe by the followers, which increases the bond of attraction between them." This seems to suggest that charisma is a leadership technique. See also Alan Bryman, *Charisma and Leadership in Organizations* (Newbury, CA: Sage Publications, 1992), 22: "the term is often employed to describe someone who is flamboyant, who is a powerful speaker, and who can persuade others of the importance of his or her message."

2. See the following references to Paul's letter to the Corinthians: 1 Cor 12:1; 1 Cor 2:12; 1 Cor 14:12; 1 Cor 12:7; 1 Cor 7:7.

3. See 1 Cor 12:8–10; 28–30; Rom 12:2–8; Eph 4:11.

4. For more detailed analysis of Paul's teachings on charisms, see Helen Doohan, *Paul's Vision of Church* (Wilmington, DE: Michael Glazier, 1989), 158, and Helen Doohan, *The Corinthian Correspondence: Ministering in the Best and Worst of Times* (San Jose, CA: Resource Publications, 1996), 98–100.

5. See Matt 10:24–25; 23:11–12; Rom 12:6–8.

6. For more on discernment of spirits in Paul, see Helen Doohan, *Paul's Vision of Church*, 127–29.

7. Bruce Malina is the writer, but I have been unable to find the specific reference.

8. Bryman, *Charisma and Leadership*, 29, quotes Weber speaking about the incompatibility of charismatic leadership and bureaucratic organizations with the prospect of the "castration of charisma" by the organization. He also quotes Givant, 31–32, about "pseudo charisma"

and fake charisma, achieved through stage management and advertising rather than personal qualities.

9. See R. Harvanck, "The Expectations of Leadership," *Way* 15 (1975): 32–33.

10. For added ideas on the characteristics of a charismatic leader, see Bruce J. Avolio and Bernard M. Bass, "Transformational Leadership, Charisma and Beyond," in *Emerging Leadership Vistas*, James G. Hunt and others, eds. (Lexington, KY: Lexington Books, 1988), 38; Jay A. Conger, "Charismatic and Transformational Leadership in Organizations: An Insider's Perspective on these Developing Streams of Research," *Leadership Quarterly* 10 (1999): 145–79.

11. Edgar H. Schein, "Leadership Competencies: A Provocative New Look," in *The Leader of the Future 2: New Visions, Strategies, and Practices for the Next Era*, Frances Hesselbein and Marshall Goldsmith, eds. (San Francisco: Jossey-Bass, 2006), 255–64. The author suggests a leader should think like an anthropologist, have the skills of a family therapist, and cultivate and trust artistic instincts. By these he means be conscious of cultural variations and be culturally humble, follow the health of an organization and understand anxiety and defense mechanisms, and be open to artistic stimulation as well as conceptual and emotional stimulations.

12. Kaiser, *The Road Ahead*, 2.

13. Greenleaf, "The Leadership Crisis," 304.

14. See Urban Holmes, *A History of Christian Spirituality* (New York: Seabury Press, 1981), 99.

15. See Bennis and Nanus, *Leaders*, 27, where they quote T. E. Lawrence. "All men dream; but not equally. Those who dream by night in the dusty recesses of their minds awake to find that it was vanity; but the dreamers of day are dangerous men, that they may act their dreams with open eyes to make it possible."

16. See James A. Belasco and Ralph C. Stayer, *Flight of the Buffalo: Soaring to Excellence, Learning to Let Employees Lead* (New York: Warner Books Inc., 1993), 202.

17. Boland, "Hope," 401–3.

18. Judy B. Rosener, "Ways Women Lead," *Harvard Business Review* 68 (Nov.–Dec. 1990): 120.

19. See Leonard Doohan, *Spiritual Leadership*, 39–41.

20. Koestenbaum, *Leadership*, 91.

CHAPTER SIX

1. See Rick Ginsberg and Timothy Gray Davies, *The Human Side of Leadership: Navigating Emotions at Work* (Westport, CT: Praeger, 2007), 22–25.

2. J. W. McLean and William Weitzel, *Leadership: Magic, Myth, or Method* (New York: AMACOM, 1992), 26. See also John Edwin Mroz, "Leadership over Fear," in *The Leader of the Future 2: New Visions, Strategies, and Practices for the Next Era*, Frances Hesselbein and Marshall Goldsmith, eds. (San Francisco: Jossey-Bass, 2006), 109.

3. See Ann McGee Cooper with Duane Trammell and Gary Looper, "Servant Leadership: Reflections on a 30 Year Partnership of the Spirit," *International Journal of Servant Leadership* 2 (2006): 300.

4. See Bernard J. Tyrrell, *Christotherapy: Healing through Enlightenment* (New York: Seabury Press, 1975).

5. See Ginsberg and Davies, *The Human Side of Leadership*, 91–97, where they give twelve lessons for planning one's emotional reactions at work. 1. Accept that leadership involves emotional experiences. 2. Be prepared. 3. Take care of yourself. 4. Become emotionally sensitive to others. 5. Be aware of the emotional potholes. 6. Be willing to change. 7. Own your own expressions. 8. Don't panic. 9. Be persistent. 10. Become emotionally aware. 11. Learn to regulate your emotions. 12. Develop your personal emotional plan.

6. In his Gospel, Matthew quotes Jesus as saying, "For out of the heart come evil thoughts....these are what defile a man" (Matt 15:19–20).

7. Usman A. Ghani calls the kind of leader who can do this a "leader integrator," and lists the most important characteristics of such a leader, including faith in the power of an idea, deep listening to

multiple perspectives, openness to critique, creative decision making, bridge building, visionary with limitless perspectives, continuous learning, and developing other leaders. See Usman A. Ghani, "The Leader Integrator: An Emerging Role," in *The Leader of the Future 2: New Visions, Strategies, and Practices for the Next Era*, Frances Hesselbein and Marshall Goldsmith, eds. (San Francisco: Jossey-Bass, 2006), 241–53.

8. John C. Knapp, "Leadership, Accountability, and the Deficit of Public Trust," in *The Ethics of Leadership in the 21st Century*, John C. Knapp, ed. (Westport, CT: Praeger, 2007), 33.

9. Kouze and Posner, "It's Not Just the Leader's Vision," 212.

10. See Stephen R. Covey, *Principled Centered Leadership* (New York: Simon and Schuster, 1992), chapter 7, "Seven Deadly Sins," 87–93.

11. See Ted W. Egstrom, *The Making of a Christian Leader* (Grand Rapids: Zondervan, 1976), 125.

12. Robert W. Terry, *Authentic Leadership: Courage in Action* (San Francisco: Jossey-Bass, 1993), 40.

CHAPTER SEVEN

1. Lynn Barendsen and Howard Gardner, "The Three Elements of Good Leadership in Rapidly Changing Times," in *The Leader of the Future 2: New Visions, Strategies, and Practices for the Next Era*, Frances Hesselbein and Marshall Goldsmith, eds. (San Francisco: Jossey-Bass, 2006), 275.

2. John Alexander, "The Challenge of Complexity," in *The Leader of the Future 2: New Visions, Strategies, and Practices for the Next Era*, Frances Hesselbein and Marshall Goldsmith, eds. (San Francisco: Jossey-Bass, 2006), 93.

3. John of the Cross, "Spiritual Canticle," 11:1, 2.

4. See Darlyne Bailey, "Leading from the Spirit," in *The Leader of the Future 2: New Visions, Strategies, and Practices for the Next Era*, Frances Hesselbein and Marshall Goldsmith, eds. (San Francisco: Jossey-Bass, 2006), 297–303, where the author gives seven core les-

sons that can be drawn from the essence of spiritual leaders: the wisdom of authenticity, the power of humility, the self-knowledge of empathy, the balance of courage and compassion, the understanding of faith, the reflection of patience, and the transcendence of love.

5. Once again I repeat that these skills are not instead of the basic leadership abilities that everyone must have. See Bennis and Nanus, *Leaders*, 198: "This theme kept recurring in our discussions with ninety CEOs; intuitive judgment by the leader is essential, but it is effective only if it has been preceded by thorough analysis." In his *Republic*, Plato chose as leader the philosopher king.

6. Rosabeth Moss Kanter, "Creating the Culture for Innovation," in *Leading for Innovation and Organizing for Results*, Frances Hesselbein, Marshall Goldsmith, and Iain Sommerville, eds. (San Francisco: Jossey-Bass, 2002), 73.

7. James A. Ritscher, "Spiritual Leadership," 66, in *Transforming Leadership: From Vision to Results*, John D. Adams, ed. (Alexandria, VA: Miles River Press, 1986).

8. Kaiser, *The Road Ahead*, 2.

9. Harper, *The Forward-Focused Organization*, 108.

10. Harper, *The Forward-Focused Organization*, 76.

11. See Matt 13:52. The emphasis on new before old is interesting, since in normal speech those two concepts would be reversed. A wise leader first looks to the future but keeps his or her eyes on the past.

12. Bolman and Deal, *The Wizard and the Warrior*, 94–146.

13. Barendsen and Gardner, "The Three Elements of Good Leadership," 266: The best leaders have three distinct meanings of good: 1. An excellent technical and professional quality and competence; 2. an ethical orientation; and 3. a completely engaged sense of fulfillment and meaningfulness.

14. Richard O. Wolfe, *Synergy: Increasing Productivity with People, Ideas, and Things* (Dubuque, IO: Kendall/Hunt, 1993), 24.

15. Richard L. Daft and Robert H. Lengel, *Fusion Leadership:*

Unlocking the Subtle Forces That Change People and Organizations (San Francisco: Berrett-Koehler, 1998), 15.

16. See Erik R. Peterson, "Scanning More Distant Horizons," in *The Ethics of Leadership in the 21st Century*, John C. Knapp, ed. (Westport, CT: Praeger, 2007), 20.

17. Michael Maccoby, *Leader: A New Face for American Management* (New York: Simon and Schuster, 1981), 225.

18. See Kouzes and Posner, *Credibility*, 225, where they quote R. J. Sternberg and S. Grajek, "The Nature of Love," *Journal of Personality and Social Psychology* 47, no. 2 (1984): 327.

19. De Pree, *Leadership Is an Art*, 16.

20. Dorothy Marcic, *Managing with the Wisdom of Love: Uncovering Virtue in People and Organizations* (San Francisco: Jossey-Bass, 1995), 39–47.

21. See Karl E. Weick, "Leadership as the Legitimization of Doubt," in *The Future of Leadership* (San Francisco: Jossey-Bass, 2001), 94–96.

22. Kofman and Senge, "Communities of Commitment," 19.

23. Bennis and Nanus, *Leaders*, 74: "Criticism is a frequent by-product of significant actions. Receptivity to criticism is as necessary as it is loathsome. It tests the foundations of positive self-regard as does nothing else. And the more valid the criticism, the more difficult it is to receive."

24. See Leonard Doohan, *Spiritual Leadership*, 38–43.

25. John W. Gardner, *On Leadership* (New York: The Free Press, 1990), 127.

CHAPTER EIGHT

1. Kofman and Senge, "Communities of Commitment," 22.

2. Handy and Bennis, *The Age of Unreason*, 11.

3. Marcic, *Managing with the Wisdom of Love*, 113.

4. See Geoffrey M. Bellman, *Getting Things Done When You Are Not in Charge* (San Francisco: Berrett-Koehler, 1992), 79–81. Bellman

offers the following suggestions for creating a positive climate: 1. Deal with people face to face. 2. Find shared goals. 3. Take the larger, longer view. 4. Take an open, receptive stance. 5. Use openness to undermine secretive, back-room politics. 6. Increase your tolerance of ambiguity. 7. Remember that understanding does not mean agreement.

5. See Dennis T. Jaffe, Cynthia D. Scott, and Glenn R. Tobe, *Rekindling Commitment: How to Revitalize Yourself, Your Work, and Your Organization* (San Francisco: Jossey-Bass, 1994), 49.

6. See David L. Dotlich and Peter C. Cairo, *Unnatural Leadership: Ten New Leadership Instincts* (San Francisco: Jossey-Bass, 2002). Their book develops ten instincts. 1. Refuse to be a prisoner of experience. 2. Expose your vulnerabilities. 3. Acknowledge your shadow side. 4. Develop a right-versus-right decision-making mentality. 5. Create teams that create discomfort. 6. Trust others before they earn it. 7. Coach and teach rather than lead and inspire. 8. Connect instead of create. 9. Give up some control. 10. Challenge the conventional wisdom.

7. De Pree, *Leadership Is an Art*, 24.

8. Stephen R. Covey, "The Ideal Community," in *The Community of the Future*, Frances Hesselbein, Marshall Goldsmith, Richard Beckhard, and Richard F. Schubert, eds. (San Francisco: Jossey-Bass, 1998), 54.

9. Leonard Doohan, *Spiritual Leadership*, 93–95.

10. Joseph A. Maciariello, "Peter F. Drucker on Executive Leadership and Effectiveness," in *The Leader of the Future 2: New Visions, Strategies, and Practices for the Next Era*, Frances Hesselbein and Marshall Goldsmith, eds. (San Francisco: Jossey-Bass, 2006), 6.

11. Peter Senge, "Leadership in Living Organizations," in *Leading Beyond the Walls*, Frances Hesselbein, Marshall Goldsmith, and Ian Somerville, eds. (San Francisco: Jossey-Bass, 1999), 77.

12. Leonard Doohan, *Spiritual Leadership*, 95–100.

13. For detailed description of a collaborative organization, see my book *Grass Roots Pastors*, chapter 2, "Collaboration."

14. Kofman, "Communities of Commitment," 16.

15. See Greenleaf, *Servant Leadership*, 244: "Followership is an equally responsible role because it means that the individual must take the risk to empower the leader and to say that, in the matter at hand, I will trust your insight."

16. See John F. Magee, "Decision Trees for Decision Making," *Harvard Business Review* 42 (1964): 135, where the author quotes Peter F. Drucker.

17. See Warren Bennis, Gretchen M. Spreitzer, and Thomas G. Cummings, eds., *The Future of Leadership: Today's Top Leadership Thinkers Speak to Tomorrow's Leaders* (San Francisco: Jossey-Bass, 2001); Sally Helgesen, *The Female Advantage: Women's Ways of Leadership* (New York: Doubleday, 1989), 30; Kouzes and Posner, *The Leadership Challenge*, 93; Jennifer James, *Thinking in the Future Tense* (New York: Touchstone Books, 1996); Hesselbein, Goldsmith, and Sommerville, eds., *Leading for Innovation*; Harper, *The Forward-Focused Organization*, 105; Harlan Cleveland, *The Knowledge Executive: Leadership in an Information Society* (New York: Truman Talley Books, 1985), 165; Pulley, *Losing Your Job*, 188; Bennis and Nanus, *Leaders*, 52.

18. John Naisbitt, *Megatrends* (New York: Warner Books, 1984), 13.

19. Handy and Bennis, *The Age of Unreason*, 5.

20. Harper, *The Forward-Focused Organization*, 165.

21. Handy and Bennis, *The Age of Unreason*, 5.

22. See Harper, *The Forward-Focused Organization*, 6–7, where the author refers to seven levels of commitment to change: champions, committed, participants, observers, skeptics, overt resisters, covert resisters.

23. Bernard Cooke, *Reconciled Sinners: Healing Human Brokenness* (Mystic, CT: Twenty-Third Publications, 1986), 8.

24. Marcic, *Managing with the Wisdom of Love*, 19.

25. See James M. Kouzes and Barry Z. Posner, *Encouraging the Heart: A Leader's Guide to Rewarding and Recognizing Others* (San Francisco: Jossey-Bass, 2003), chapter 12, 151–75: "150 Ways to Encourage the Heart."

26. Maciariello, "Peter F. Drucker on Executive Leadership," 7.

27. Don E. Saliers, "Joy," in *New Dictionary of Catholic Spirituality*, Michael Downey, ed. (Collegeville, MN: Liturgical Press, 1993), 578.

CONCLUSION

1. See Marshall Goldsmith, "Leading New Age Professionals," in *The Leader of the Future 2: New Visions, Strategies, and Practices for the Next Era*, Frances Hesselbein and Marshall Goldsmith, eds. (San Francisco: Jossey-Bass, 2006), 169–72: the author speaks about a series of qualities that leaders need to pass on to others: "Encourage their passion, enhance their ability, value their time, build their network, support their dreams, and expand their contribution."

2. Robert J. Spitzer, *The Spirit of Leadership: Optimizing Creativity and Change in Organizations* (Provo, UT: EEP, 2000), 33–36: "Seven Effects of Spirit."

3. Kouzes and Posner, *Credibility*, 54.

BIBLIOGRAPHY

Adams, John D., ed. *Transforming Leadership: From Vision to Results*. Alexandria, VA: Miles River Press, 1986.

Alexander, John. "The Challenge of Complexity." In *The Leader of the Future 2: New Visions, Strategies, and Practices for the Next Era*, Frances Hesselbein and Marshall Goldsmith, eds., 85–94. San Francisco: Jossey-Bass, 2006.

Alfaro, Juan. "Christian Hope and the Hopes of Mankind." *Concilium* 59 (1970): 59–69.

Avolio, Bruce J., and Bernard M. Bass. "Transformational Leadership, Charisma and Beyond." In *Emerging Leadership Vistas*, James G. Hunt and others, eds., 29–49. Lexington, KY: Lexington Books, 1988.

Bailey, Darlyne. "Leading from the Spirit." In *The Leader of the Future 2: New Visions, Strategies, and Practices for the Next Era*, Frances Hesselbein and Marshall Goldsmith, eds., 297–303. San Francisco: Jossey-Bass, 2006.

Barendsen, Lynn, and Howard Gardner. "The Three Elements of Good Leadership in Rapidly Changing Times." In *The Leader of the Future 2: New Visions, Strategies, and Practices for the Next Era*, Frances Hesselbein and Marshall Goldsmith, eds., 265–79. San Francisco: Jossey-Bass, 2006.

Belasco, James A., and Ralph C. Stayer. *Flight of the Buffalo: Soaring to Excellence, Learning to Let Employees Lead*. New York: Warner Books Inc., 1993.

Bellman, Geoffrey M. *Getting Things Done When You Are Not in Charge*. San Francisco: Berrett-Koehler, 1992.

Bennis, Warren, and Burt Nanus. *Leaders*. New York: Harper and Row, 1985.

Bennis, Warren, Gretchen M. Spreitzer, and Thomas G. Cummings, eds. *The Future of Leadership: Today's Top Leadership Thinkers Speak to Tomorrow's Leaders.* San Francisco: Jossey-Bass, 2001.

Boland, Vivian. "Hope." In *Modern Catholic Encyclopedia,* Michael Glazier and Monika Hellwig, eds., 401–3. Collegeville, MN: Liturgical Press, 1994.

Bolman, Lee G., and Terrence E. Deal. *Leading with Soul: An Uncommon Journey of Spirit.* San Francisco: Jossey-Bass, 1995.

———. *The Wizard and the Warrior: Leading with Passion and Power.* San Francisco: Jossey-Bass, 2006.

Brueggemann, Walter. *The Prophetic Imagination.* Minneapolis, MN: Fortress Press, 1987.

Bryman, Alan. *Charisma and Leadership in Organizations.* Newbury, CA: Sage Publications, 1992.

Cleveland, Harlan. *The Knowledge Executive: Leadership in an Information Society.* New York: Truman Talley Books, 1985.

Conger, Jay A. "Charismatic and Transformational Leadership in Organizations: An Insider's Perspective on These Developing Streams of Research." *Leadership Quarterly* 10 (1999): 145–79.

Cooke, Bernard. *Reconciled Sinners: Healing Human Brokenness.* Mystic, CT: Twenty-Third Publications, 1986.

Covey, Stephen R. "The Ideal Community." In *The Community of the Future,* Frances Hesselbein, Marshall Goldsmith, Richard Beckhard, and Richard F. Schubert, eds. San Francisco: Jossey-Bass, 1998.

———. *Principled Centered Leadership.* New York: Simon and Schuster, 1992.

———. *7 Habits of Highly Effective People: Restoring the Character Ethic.* New York: Simon and Schuster, 1989.

———. "Three Roles of the Leader in the New Paradigm." In *The Leader of the Future: New Visions, Stategies, and Practices for the Next Era,* Frances Hesselbein, Marshall Goldsmith, and Richard Beckhard, eds., 149–59. San Francisco: Jossey-Bass, 1996.

Cronin, Thomas E. "Reflections on Leadership." In *Contemporary Issues in Leadership*, William E. Rosenbach and Robert L. Taylor, eds., 21–23. San Francisco: Westview Press, 1993.

Daft, Richard L., and Robert H. Lengel. *Fusion Leadership: Unlocking the Subtle Forces That Change People and Organizations*. San Francisco: Berrett-Koehler, 1998.

Demaison, Michael. "The Christian Utopia." *Concilium* 59 (1970): 42–58.

De Pree, Max. *Leadership Is an Art*. Lansing, MI: Michigan State University Press, 1987.

Doohan, Helen. *The Corinthian Correspondence: Ministering in the Best and Worst of Times*. San Jose, CA: Resource Publications, 1996.

———. *Paul's Vision of Church*. Wilmington, DE: Michael Glazier, 1989.

Doohan, Leonard. *Grass Roots Pastors*. San Francisco: Harper and Row, 1986.

———. *Spiritual Leadership: The Quest for Integrity*. New York/Mahwah, NJ: Paulist Press, 2007.

Dotlich, David L., and Peter C. Cairo. *Unnatural Leadership: Ten New Leadership Instincts*. San Francisco: Jossey-Bass, 2002.

Downey, John. "The Future of Political Theology." *Horizons* 34, no. 2 (2007): 306–28.

Downey, John, ed. *Love's Strategy: The Political Theology of Johann Baptist Metz*. Harrisburg, PA: Trinity Press International, 1999.

Eggert, Nancy J. *Contemplative Leadership for Entrepreneurial Organizations*. Westport, CT: Quorum Books, 1998.

Egstrom, Ted W. *The Making of a Christian Leader*. Grand Rapids: Zondervan, 1976.

Gardner, John W. *On Leadership*. New York: The Free Press, 1990.

Ghani, Usman A. "The Leader Integrator: An Emerging Role." In *The Leader of the Future 2: New Visions, Strategies, and Practices for the Next Era*, Frances Hesselbein and Marshall Goldsmith, eds., 241–53. San Francisco: Jossey-Bass, 2006.

Ginsberg, Rick, and Timothy Gray Davies. *The Human Side of Leadership: Navigating Emotions at Work*. Westport, CT: Praeger, 2007.

Goldsmith, Marshall. "Leading New Age Professionals." In *The Leader of the Future 2: New Visions, Strategies, and Practices for the Next Era*, Frances Hesselbein and Marshall Goldsmith, eds., 169–72. San Francisco: Jossey-Bass, 2006.

———. *What Got You Here Won't Get You There*. New York: Hyperion Books, 2007.

Golford, Robert, and Anne Siebold Drapeau. *The Trusted Leader*. New York: The Free Press, 2002.

Greenleaf, Robert K. *Servant Leadership: A Journey into the Nature of Legitimate Power and Greatness*. New York: Paulist Press, 1977.

———. "The Leadership Crisis." *Humanitas* 14 (1978): 296–306.

Greer, Rowan A. *Christian Hope and Christian Life*. New York: Crossroad Publishing Co., 2001.

Hammerskjold, Dag. *Markings*. New York: Knopf, 1964.

Handy, Charles, and Warren Bennis. *The Age of Unreason*. Boston: Harvard Business School Press, 1990.

Häring, Bernard. *Theology of Protest*. New York: Farrar, Straus and Giroux, 1970.

Harper, Stephen C. *The Forward-Focused Organization: Visionary Thinking and Breakthrough Leadership to Create Your Company's Future*. New York: AMACOM, 2001.

Harvanck, R. "The Expectations of Leadership." *Way* 15 (1975): 32–33.

Hawley, Jack. *Reawakening the Spirit in Work: The Power of Dharmic Management*. San Francisco: Berrett-Koehler, 1993.

Helgesen, Sally. *The Female Advantage: Women's Ways of Leadership*. New York: Doubleday, 1989.

Hellwig, Monika. "Hope." In *The New Dictionary of Catholic Spirituality*, Michael Downey, ed., 506–15. Collegeville, MN: Liturgical Press, 1993.

Hesselbein, Frances, and Marshall Goldsmith, eds. *The Leader of the Future 2: New Visions, Strategies, and Practices for the Next Era*. San Francisco: Jossey-Bass, 2006.

Hesselbein, Frances, Marshall Goldsmith, and Richard Beckhard, eds. *The Leader of the Future: New Visions, Strategies, and Practices for the Next Era*. San Francisco: Jossey-Bass, 1996.

Hesselbein, Frances, Marshall Goldsmith, Richard Beckhard, and Richard F. Schubert, eds. *The Community of the Future*. San Francisco: Jossey-Bass, 1998.

Hesselbein, Frances, Marshall Goldsmith, and Iain Somerville, eds. *Leading Beyond the Walls*. San Francisco: Jossey-Bass, 1999.

———. *Leading for Innovation and Organizing for Results*. San Francisco: Jossey-Bass, 2002.

Holmes, Urban. *A History of Christian Spirituality*. New York: Seabury Press, 1981.

Hunt, James G., and others, eds. *Emerging Leadership Vistas*. Lexington, KY: Lexington Books, 1988.

Jaffe, Dennis T., Cynthia D. Scott, and Glenn R. Tobe. *Rekindling Commitment: How to Revitalize Yourself, Your Work, and Your Organization*. San Francisco: Jossey-Bass, 1994.

James, Jennifer. *Thinking in the Future Tense*. New York: Touchstone Books, 1996.

John of the Cross. *The Collected Works of St. John of the Cross*. Translated by Kieran Kavanaugh, OCD, and Otilio Rodriguez, OCD. Washington, DC: ICS Publications, 1979.

Kaiser, Leland. *The Road Ahead—Transform Yourself, Your Organization, and Your Community*. Englewood, CO: Estes Park Institute Notes, 1998.

Kersteins, Ferdinand. "Hope." In *Sacramentum Mundi*, vol. 3, Karl Rahner and others, eds., 61–65. London: Burns and Oates, 1968.

158

————. "The Theology of Hope in Germany Today." *Concilium* 59 (1970): 110–11.

Khare, R. S., and David Little. *Leadership*. University Press of America, 1984.

Knapp, John C. "Leadership, Accountability, and the Deficit of Public Trust." In *The Ethics of Leadership in the 21st Century*, John C. Knapp, ed., 33–41. Westport, CT: Praeger, 2007.

Knapp, John C., ed. *The Ethics of Leadership in the 21st Century*. Westport, CT: Praeger, 2007.

Koestenbaum, Peter. *Leadership: The Inner Side of Greatness*. San Francisco: Jossey-Bass, 1991.

Kofman, Fred, and Peter M. Senge. "Communities of Commitment: The Heart of Learning Organizations." *Organizational Dynamics* 21 (Autumn 1993): 5–23.

Kouzes, James M., and Barry Z. Posner. *Credibility: How Leaders Gain and Lose It, Why People Demand It*. San Francisco: Jossey-Bass, 1993.

————. *Encouraging the Heart: A Leader's Guide to Rewarding and Recognizing Others*. San Francisco: Jossey-Bass, 2003.

————. "It's Not Just the Leader's Vision." In *The Leader of the Future 2: Visions, Strategies, and Practices for the Next Era*, Frances Hesselbein and Marshall Goldsmith, eds., 207–21. San Francisco: Jossey-Bass, 2006.

————. *The Leadership Challenge: How to Get Extraordinary Things Done in Organizations*. San Francisco: Jossey-Bass, 1988.

————. "Seven Lessons for Leading the Voyage to the Future." In *The Leader of the Future*, Frances Hesselbein, Marshall Goldsmith, and Richard Beckhard, eds., 99–110. San Francisco: Jossey-Bass, 1996.

Lane, Dermot A. *Keeping Hope Alive: Stirrings in Christian Theology*. New York: Paulist Press, 1996.

Maccoby, Michael. *Leader: A New Face for American Management*. New York: Simon and Schuster, 1981.

Maciariello, Joseph A. "Peter F. Drucker on Executive Leadership and Effectiveness." In *The Leader of the Future 2: New Visions, Strategies, and Practices for the Next Era*, Frances Hesselbein and Marshall Goldsmith, eds., 3–27. San Francisco: Jossey-Bass, 2006.

Magee, John F. "Decision Trees for Decision Making." *Harvard Business Review* 42 (1964): 126–38.

Marcic, Dorothy. *Managing with the Wisdom of Love: Uncovering Virtue in People and Organizations*. San Francisco: Jossey-Bass, 1995.

Markam, Donna J. *Spiritlinking Leadership: Working through Resistance to Organizational Change*. New York: Paulist Press, 1999.

McBrien, Richard P. *Catholicism*. Vol. II. Minneapolis, MN: Winston Press, 1980.

———. *Church: The Continuing Quest*. New York: Newman Press, 1970.

McGee-Cooper, Ann, Duane Trammell, and Gary Looper. "Servant Leadership: Reflections on a 30 Year Partnership of the Spirit." *International Journal of Servant Leadership* 2 (2006): 297–315.

McLean, J. W., and William Weitzel. *Leadership: Magic, Myth, or Method?* New York: AMACOM, 1992.

Messer, Donald E. *Contemporary Images of Christian Ministry*. Nashville: Abingdon Press, 1989.

Minear, Paul. *To Heal and to Reveal: The Prophetic Vision According to Luke*. New York: Seabury Press, 1976.

Moltmann, Jürgen. *In the End—the Beginning: The Life of Hope*. Minneapolis, MN: Fortress Press, 2004.

———. "Theology as Eschatology." In *The Future of Hope*, Jürgen Moltmann and others, eds., 1–50. New York: Herder and Herder, 1970.

———. *Theology of Hope*. San Francisco: Harper and Row, 1967.

Moss Kanter, Rosabeth. "Creating the Culture for Innovation." In *Leading for Innovation and Organizing for Results*, Frances Hesselbein, Marshall Goldsmith, and Iain Somerville, eds., 73–85. San Francisco: Jossey-Bass, 2002.

Mroz, John Edwin. "Leadership over Fear." In *The Leader of the Future 2: New Visions, Strategies, and Practices for the Next Era*, Frances Hesselbein and Marshall Goldsmith, eds., 107–20. San Francisco: Jossey-Bass, 2006.

Naisbitt, John. *Megatrends*. New York: Warner Books, 1984.

Nanus, Burt. *Visionary Leadership: Creating a Compelling Sense of Direction for Your Organization*. San Francisco: Jossey-Bass, 1992.

Owen, Harrison. *The Spirit of Leadership: Liberating the Leader in Each of Us*. San Francisco: Berrett-Koehler, 1999.

Peterson, Erik R. "Scanning More Distant Horizons." In *The Ethics of Leadership in the 21st Century*, John C. Knapp, ed., 3–20. Westport, CT: Praeger, 2007.

Pulley, Mary. *Losing Your Job—Reclaiming Your Spirit: Stories of Resilience, Renewal, and Hope*. San Francisco: Jossey-Bass, 1997.

Ramey, David A. *Empowering Leaders*. Kansas City: Sheed and Ward, 1991.

Ritscher, James A. "Spiritual Leadership." In *Transforming Leadership: From Vision to Results*, John D. Adams, ed., 1–80. Alexandria, VA: Miles River Press, 1986.

Rosener, Judy B. "Ways Women Lead." *Harvard Business Review* 68 (Nov.-Dec. 1990): 119–25.

Russell, Letty M. *Changing Contexts of Our Faith*. Philadelphia: Fortress Press, 1985.

Saliers, Don E. "Joy." In *New Dictionary of Catholic Spirituality*, Michael Downey, ed., 577–78. Collegeville, MN: Liturgical Press, 1993.

Schein, Edgar H. "Leadership Competencies: A Provocative New Look." In *The Leader of the Future 2: New Visions, Strategies, and Practices for the Next Era*, Frances Hesselbein and Marshall Goldsmith, eds., 255–64. San Francisco: Jossey-Bass, 2006.

Scanlon, Michael. "Hope." In *New Dictionary of Theology*, Joseph Komonchak, Mary Collins, and Dermot A. Lane, eds., 492–98. Collegeville, MN: Liturgical Press, 1987.

Courageous Hope

Scott, R. B. Y. *The Relevance of the Prophets*. New York: Macmillan, 1944.

Senge, Peter. "Leadership in Living Organizations." In *Leading Beyond the Walls*, Frances Hesselbein, Marshall Goldsmith, and Iain Somerville, eds., 73–90. San Francisco: Jossey-Bass, 1999.

———. "Systems Citizenship: The Leadership Mandate for this Millennium." In *The Leader of the Future 2: New Visions, Strategies, and Practices for the Next Era*, Frances Hesselbein and Marshall Goldsmith, eds., 31–46. San Francisco: Jossey-Bass, 2006.

Shriberg, Arthur, Carol Lloyd, David L. Shriberg, and Mary Lynn Williamson. *Practicing Leadership: Principles and Applications*. New York: John Wiley and Sons, 1997.

Spitzer, Robert J. *The Spirit of Leadership: Optimizing Creativity and Change in Organizations*. Provo, UT: EEP, 2000.

Terry, Robert W. *Authentic Leadership: Courage in Action*. San Francisco: Jossey-Bass, 1993.

Tyrrell, Bernard J. *Christotherapy: Healing through Enlightenment*. New York: Seabury Press, 1975.

Weick, Karl E. "Leadership as the Legitimization of Doubt." In *The Future of Leadership*, Warren Bennis, Gretchen M. Spreitzer, and Thomas G. Cummings, eds., 91–103. San Francisco: Jossey-Bass, 2001.

Wolfe, Richard O. *Synergy: Increasing Productivity with People, Ideas, and Things*. Dubuque, IA: Kendall/Hunt, 1993.

Yukl, Gary A. *Leadership in Organizations*. Upper Saddle River, NJ: Prentice Hall, 1989.